Perspectives on Implementation

MENC · Music Educators National Conference

Perspectives on Implementation

Arts Education Standards for America's Students

Edited by Bruce O. Boston

 Music Educators National Conference

Developed by the Arts Standards Implementation Task Force
under a grant from the John D. and Catherine T. MacArthur Foundation
and the Geraldine R. Dodge Foundation,
administered by Music Educators National Conference.

Project Director: John J. Mahlmann
Project Administrator: Mary Ann Cameron

Published by Music Educators National Conference
in cooperation with
American Alliance for Theatre & Education
National Art Education Association
National Dance Association

Contents

Preface

During the development of the National Standards for Arts Education, the Music Educators National Conference, in cooperation with the American Alliance for Theatre & Education, the National Art Education Association, and the National Dance Association, began to think seriously about the issues and strategies involved in the implementation of these Standards at the state and local levels. With the support and guidance of the John D. and Catherine T. MacArthur Foundation and the Geraldine R. Dodge Foundation, a task force was assembled to examine the complexities of implementation from different perspectives.

Five task force members were chosen for their experience and expertise in advocacy, professional development, opportunity-to-learn standards, disciplinary connections, and assessment; and seven were chosen to represent the constituencies that will be involved in Standards implementation—parents, administrators, school boards, the arts community, business, state agencies, and state legislatures.

The task force was assisted by a review board composed of teachers and other education leaders. Thus, this book reflects the concerns of key players in American education.

It is hoped that this initial effort will provoke discussion and provide a valuable foundation for an ongoing process of improving the quality of education for all of America's students.

Introduction

When the year 2000 finally arrives, what are the chances that any or all of the following scenarios will accurately describe a typical high school graduate in the United States?

♦ Maria will be able to reflect on, interpret, and critically assess the characteristics and qualities of a painting she has never seen before, and use what she has discovered to develop her own painting technique.

♦ John will have the basic acting skills needed to portray characters in scripted and improvised scenes, drawn from both American and, say, French culture.

♦ Trinh will be able to sight-read and sing his tenor part in an eighteenth-century choral work. When that is done, he will be able to do the same for a work that a classmate has just composed.

♦ Joanne will be able to create a time line that traces the history of the important events in the development of dance in the twentieth century and place those events in their proper social and political contexts. She will be able to apply the same intellectual technique to dances of other periods.

The knowledge and skills described here are drawn from the National Standards for Arts Education, released in early 1994. The Standards outline "what students should know and be able to do" in the arts when they complete the fourth, eighth, and twelfth grades. If adopted and implemented by the states, these scenarios—and many like them—will not be hypothetical; they will be real.

Why is this important? First, the arts represent one of the primary modes of thought used to do essential work in the world at large. Creative thinking is based in artistic methods. For example, the methods of art convert scientific knowledge into technology. Second, our dances, our music, our visual environment, and our movies, videos, and staged productions all produce the cultural context for everything else. The arts exert influences on society as profound as our scientific discoveries, our histori-

1

cal understandings, or our economic and political aspirations. In fact, the arts are often the means for expressing and explaining these other things. Third, the arts represent a legacy of human achievement, a precious heritage of civilization that teaches us about ourselves and others. Study of the arts also produces personal benefits, engaging students with work that encourages self-motivation, self-discipline, cooperation, productivity, and thus, self-esteem. There is a growing body of evidence that substantive arts study promotes achievement in other subjects and on standardized tests.

In light of all these reasons, let us look at Maria, John, Trinh, and Joanne again. Their ability to do complex operations in the arts results from study that involves the art forms for what they do, what they mean, and what they are. The specific skills noted testify to the broader competence the Standards seek to develop.

But the Standards are voluntary, and therein lies the challenge around which this book is organized. Because the constitutional responsibility for education in the United States is left to the states, the option of imposing education standards from some central ministry of education does not exist in this country; local control is the rule. At the same time, many reform experiments rooted in models of local control have fallen short of their original promise; taxpayers are unsure whether the schools can deliver. In addition, too many American children, especially those from poor families, are receiving a substandard education. Local problems and variations in quality have thus caused many states to take a stronger stand for educational reform, particularly by implementing more rigorous curricula and forms of assessment. Education standards are seen by many as a way of sharpening the teeth of education reform, of going beyond organizational issues to the very heart of the subjects our children study in school.

Why Standards?

The push for standards grew out of the National Governors Conference in 1989, which established national education goals. Goal Three called for students to demonstrate their competency in challenging subject matter. The arts are now one of the major subject areas considered to be part of a "basic" education and for which standards are being drawn up. The Goals 2000: Educate America Act furthers the Standards effort by establishing the National Education Standards Improvement Council to officially endorse education standards that meet defined criteria. In addition, the legislation proposes a partnership between federal, state, and local education agencies to provide incentives for curriculum design and assessment plans.

But why do we need education standards in general—and arts standards in particular? There are many reasons. One broad reason is that in a highly competitive world, the well-being of the people of every nation rests on their ability to compete, not just economically but intellectually. When American students rank outside the top ten on international comparisons of achievement in math and science—as they have—they are entering the global work force at a disadvantage and their own future is threatened. Education standards address that situation directly.

But the issue isn't the results of the measurement. The real issue is what kind of learning goes on (or doesn't go on) to produce the measured result. Perhaps an athletic analogy will help. A sprinter is measured in a race by a stopwatch. But that performance depends on moving through a graduated set of requirements to become a strong runner: innumerable training races, stretching exercises, punishing uphill sprints, a weight-training program, a specific diet, and the like. The sprinter's time symbolizes the result of that process. Similarly, with requirements established to define and develop a child's knowledge and skills, no matter the area of study, *measurable* progress can occur. Education standards are simply statements of what we believe children should know and be able to do at specific points in the course of their education.

Another important reason for having education standards is that without them, there is no realistic way to improve teaching or learning. Unless we say, "By such-and-such a time, a child will know this and be able to do that," there is no way of determining if either our children, or the schools they go to, are doing the job we want them to do. And indeed, voicing "what we want them to do" is only a different way of expressing a standard.

A third reason for setting education standards is that they establish expectations. Much educational research now points in the direction of a commonsense observation: children will work to the level of expectation that is put before them. Standards are a formal way of taking advantage of this fact and turning it to the child's long-range advantage.

All academic subjects require standards of some kind to help determine a student's progress, whether in English, history, geography, or the arts. Standards are necessary in the arts, specifically, because the arts are fully as rigorous, academically, as any other area. They make a difference in the way the arts are studied by defining the goals carefully. The National Standards for Arts Education insist that an education in the arts be a comprehensive, sequenced enterprise of learning across the four arts disciplines (dance, music, theatre, the visual arts); and that students be grounded in knowledge, disciplinary skills, techniques, and particularly the thinking skills that infuse the arts, and, in short, that both quality and accountability be factored into this vital area of education.

Beyond this reasoning, the rationale behind the recent movement to establish subject-area standards in American education has created a window of opportunity for the arts to be established as an integral part of the core curriculum for *all* students. This development will greatly enhance the prospect that future high school graduates will be more like Maria, John, Trinh, and Joanne—able to meet specific criteria in the study of dance, music, theatre, and the visual arts. But the prospect that their scenarios will become reality in the schools are dim unless the arts education Standards are, in fact, implemented.

Successful implementation rests first with the people who developed these Standards—arts educators and the arts community. They have built a strong foundation. Because of their past and present hard work, other groups will be able to join the implementation effort, and students will be able to meet the levels the Standards require. Dedicated teachers and advocates in the arts community have the power to persuade parents, school boards, state education agencies, legislative bodies, and business leaders of the importance of the arts to a well-rounded education and a meaningful life. With that said, however, implementation of the Standards faces formidable barriers.

Barriers to Implementation

Although we often speak loosely of "the American education system," what we have is not a "system" at all, but a collection of some fifteen thousand school districts operating under local control and according to local traditions, all under a complex umbrella of state and federal laws, regulations, and policies. Because the arts are often viewed as an educational frill, they have not enjoyed a secure position in many schools and districts, or in the mind of

the public, when it comes to defining what is important in education. Among the most formidable barriers to implementing the Standards for arts education, then, is *limited public knowledge* about the arts and the value and benefits of arts education.

Overcoming this barrier will involve a good deal more than simply passing out copies of the Standards. Even when parents and teachers have information, they are unlikely to use it unless it is easy to understand, there are incentives involved, and there is plenty of time to discuss, analyze, and get answers to questions. Meeting this difficulty will require a well-orchestrated program of information and advocacy involving all elements of the education and arts communities.

Assessment, an integral part of educational accountability, will also be a barrier. This issue is further complicated by the emergence of student performance assessment as a tool for improving teaching. Here, however, is one area in which arts educators have more experience than teachers in other academic areas. The assessment of performance in the form of auditions and portfolios has a long history in arts education. But that still leaves unanswered the question of comparability: How can you reliably assess student performances that are comparable among students, schools, and districts? Here, there are no quick or easy answers.

Then, there is *time.* Instructional time in every school is a precious commodity, and adoption of the various sets of academic standards now under preparation, with their qualitative implications, will place a tremendous time burden on teachers, administrators, and students. But if the Standards are to help the arts tighten their grip on a place in the curriculum, then leadership in helping teachers and administrators envision scheduling and instructional alternatives is needed.

Policy: The Critical Question

But perhaps the central question surrounding the implementation of the Standards—also a barrier of its own kind—is the question of education policy. Because the Standards are voluntary, little by way of implementation is likely to happen in any state unless state legislatures and state departments of education say, in effect, "It is our policy that these Standards (or something like them) guide arts instruction in this state," and back that declaration with resources.

At present, however, there is a *lack of policy provisions at state and local levels* that would ensure that the arts are taught at all levels of instruction. Currently, many states have only loose requirements for the amount of time to be spent on the arts. Happily, however, the Standards themselves can form the basis for developing such policy. The requirements they set forth are very clear, and their adoption turns them into something of a policy road map for teachers and administrators.

States will play a key role in helping implement the new Standards, but it is well to recognize that their past policies have been major contributors to the serious neglect of the arts in the curriculum. If the arts do not receive more attention in the curriculum frameworks developed by the states, then the arts will fare no better under the Standards than they have already. Similarly, if the arts do not have parity with other subjects in the state's assessment policy, they will have a lower priority when it comes to the allocation of instructional resources.

What might such a policy look like? It could take its shape from five major tasks that must be accomplished if implementation is to be effective: shaping public awareness, ensuring adequate professional development, changing teacher preparation, and preparing alternatives in curriculum design and scheduling. All these tasks will need to be supported by model policy examples suitable for adoption by local school districts.

Shaping Public Awareness. As virtually every essay in this book points out, a campaign of advocacy and public awareness is utterly essential to the success of Standards implementation. State education agencies will have a major role to play here in terms of providing basic information about what the Standards are, why the arts are an essential area of academic study and not a frill, and what is needed at the building level to make the Standards effective. A few key ideas must be identified and repeatedly conveyed. Alliances with all stakeholder groups in the Standards effort must be forged, and states must take a leading role.

Ensuring Adequate Professional Development. There is no more critical issue for arts education than a teaching force able to provide instruction adequate to the Standards. Teachers now responsible for arts instruction will need continuing support to expand their knowledge and help them teach to the Standards. A professional development policy would establish realistic goals, involve trainers and professionals from the several arts disciplines, and provide the resources (for example, released time, summer institutes, curricula) to assure high-quality staff development. A longer-term policy for professional development would recognize that knowledge transfer to the classroom will require follow-up, and would provide for such follow-up.

Changing Teacher Preparation. Teacher preparation institutions will need to be assisted, as a matter of state policy, to make the transition to a world in which the Standards help determine the kind of teachers that are graduated and the adequacy of their preparation in the arts. A policy of full collaboration, including technical assistance, with such organizations as the National Office for Arts Accreditation in Higher Education, the National Council for the Accreditation of Teacher Education, the Association of Teacher Educators, the American Association of Colleges for Teacher Education, and the newly established National Board for Professional Teaching Standards could become extremely effective in pursuing this goal. Any policy initiatives in which these organizations would be involved must make clear what is being asked of them. This is not to say that a whole new teacher-preparation effort for educating arts specialists is required; it is to say that we need new approaches to using and integrating the arts into pedagogy and practice teaching.

Preparing Curriculum-Design and Scheduling Alternatives. A policy framework requires a delivery mechanism. States working to implement the Standards are more likely to succeed if they can devise concrete ways to teach the arts in the ways that the Standards ask. It is not sufficient, for example, to talk about an "interdisciplinary curriculum"; examples must be provided. Similarly, concrete examples of the kind of scheduling required to provide an arts curriculum that meets the learning requirements of the Standards will also be needed. Much of this will require states and other stakeholders in Standards implementation to "think outside the lines" on such issues as performance-based models, the role of technology, block scheduling, and interdisciplinary study, using the Standards as a constant check to ensure attention to arts content.

Evidence of Effective Policy. Some indices of progress on the policy front might include: (1) the number of local school districts that adopt curriculum policies aimed at ensuring that students at all levels receive an education in the arts that meets the Standards; (2) the number of teachers who have been provided with education and training based on the Standards; (3) the results of statewide assessments in the arts; (4) the number of students who enroll in arts courses in secondary school; and (5) the number of active state and local advocacy groups actively pursuing the policy's goals.

A Call to Action

Implementing the arts Standards will take aggressive planning and policymaking. Institutions tend to resist change, but the critical importance of the arts in the lives of citizens makes this an undertaking that must succeed. Teachers are already seeing more and more of the connections between what the arts teach and the broader knowledge and skills students need to become more effective learners. The addition of the arts to the national education goals and the promulgation of National Standards for Arts Education are only first steps. Now, the arts must become full partners in the education of all our children.

The contributions of the arts to both society and the individual are too great to countenance any attitude but boldness in securing their place in the schooling of our children. The scenarios posed in the beginning are, in the end, hopeful ones, but it is up to those who care about and believe in what arts education can accomplish to make them more than fancy; we have to make them fact.—GC

Advocacy

Getting to "How To"

Karl Bruhn

Some General Thoughts on Advocacy

"Advocacy" derives from a Latin word meaning "to speak on behalf of" or "to plead a cause." But it involves much more than that. At one level, advocacy is the process of marshaling arguments, plans, and resources (people, funds, materials) to influence decision making. That's advocacy's operational side—its outside. But people don't bother to advocate things they don't care much about; they "speak on behalf of" the things that matter to them. That's why advocacy's other side is what lies on the inside— some belief, passion, or commitment that tells an advocate not just what to do but what must be done. The first thing every advocate has to be is a believer.

In this sense, *National Standards for Arts Education* is itself an advocacy document; it espouses its own cause. Its subtitle, "What Every Young American Should Know and Be Able to Do in the Arts," points to the operational side. Permeating the Standards is also the burning conviction that achieving them is good for children, good for education, good for the community, good for the country. Any advocacy strategy for implementing the Standards, therefore, has to be grounded not only in the practical know-how it takes to get things done, but also in a deeply held conviction that what must be done is the right thing to do. In the end, any advocacy strategy for implementing the Standards will be inescapably about three things: politics, problem solving, and the "how-to" skills required to be effective.

Politics. Many associated with the arts who find talk of politics uncomfortable may wish to reflect on the phrase "the art of politics." We call politics an art because, like the arts disciplines, it proceeds by coaxing new life and meaning from often recalcitrant materials through the creative use of imagination and power. Advocating the arts Standards is a political process because they are an element of education policy, and sooner or later, all policy decisions come to someone (or some group) who is elected. Even appointed school boards are named by elected officials. What makes implementing the Standards a political issue is that doing so is—at bottom—about power, policy, and the allocation of resources.

Problem Solving. Politics is marrow to the advocacy bone, but advocacy's muscle is the skill to identify and solve problems. The need for any kind of advocacy always stems, by definition, from the presence of a competing point of view, an opponent, or some other claim on resources. Every advocacy strategy is thus built on developing the ability to persuade those with the power to decide, which in turn means being able to distinguish between the significant and the trivial, the central and the peripheral, what comes first and what comes next.

◆

A successful advocacy effort ... teaches people what work to do, how to do it, and when to do it.

◆

In the case of the arts Standards, there is no want of problems and no lack of uncertainty about the priorities of implementation. The way ahead will not always be clear. Those who implement the Standards will therefore have to proceed

on many fronts and tackle many issues simultaneously. Many of these are already identified. A partial list would surely include such issues as curriculum development, student assessment, teacher preparation and professional development, costs, parental support, and community involvement. But one distinction is important: The issues surrounding successful implementation of the Standards are related to instruction, curriculum, school organization, funding, and other aspects of delivering content. But they are not the same issues that shape the question of how to be a successful advocate. The latter form the core of this article.

Getting to "How To." Advocacy is more than developing a political strategy or sorting out tasks. Advocacy is also vitally concerned with identifying and recruiting allies, finding willing workers, and providing both with the right tools for the jobs at hand. Most important to truly successful advocacy, however, is a final step that is nearly always ignored, not least by those committed to the arts and arts education: teaching the willing how to get the job done. A successful advocacy effort does not merely convert others to a particular viewpoint. It does not merely persuade others to act. It does not merely craft a brilliant strategy. *It also teaches people what work to do, how to do it, and when to do it.*

The remainder of this article proceeds, then, from these three assumptions: (1) all advocacy is half persuasion and half politics; (2) core issues must be identified for action and solution; and (3) successful advocacy depends on developing and disseminating the tools for advocacy, assigning tasks, and teaching others how to bring tasks and tools together to get results.

Four core issues are examined below in this light. In each case, a brief description of the issue is given, an advocacy goal is offered, and strategies are suggested for achieving the goal.

Issue One: Negotiating a Key

There is a long tradition of fractiousness and "turf wars" among arts advocates and in arts education at national, state, and local levels. This history of divisiveness is a serious advocacy issue because it undercuts the ability to speak with one voice. To be sure, the infighting is as understandable as it is regrettable; arts advocates are all members of the same extended family, with strong feelings and opinions; like many families, people who care about the arts are inclined to fight over small things. But the Standards are no small thing; they offer a powerful incentive to put solo performances on hold, join the same chorus, and negotiate a key to sing in.

Why? Because the plain fact is that the Standards are unprecedented in their scope and opportunity for demonstrating that the arts belong not at the periphery of American public education but at its core. The Standards provide a rallying point that has never existed before because they demonstrate decisively that the arts are just as academically rigorous as other school subjects. Perhaps most important from an advocacy standpoint, the Standards also represent a broad

consensus about goals for students that all can endorse (with full recognition that not everyone is—or can be—100 percent satisfied); in short, they provide a once-in-a-lifetime opportunity for united action. We can't afford to blow it.

Goal. As the national discussion gets under way, the goal of the arts community should be to *speak with one voice* at national, state, and local levels. The single message that must be delivered first, with all the persistence of a salesperson trying to establish a new territory, is this: These Standards should be adopted and implemented—not merely because they are sound educational practice but because they are good for children. In pursuing that goal, my own observation is that educators listen to other educators; school boards listen to parents; legislators listen to voters. The arts community has no want of friends in any of these groups. The only issue is organizing them and equipping them to deliver the message.

The danger here is that the primary message will become weighed down with "only if" baggage; for example, "We can implement only if we do X, Y, or Z first." The sure result of that kind of thinking is that the Standards will die the death of a thousand qualifications at state and local levels. Speaking with one voice means a united arts community generating a resounding "Yes" to the Standards first, then turning its attention and resources to the issues that affirmation may uncover.

Strategies. The strategic package that can achieve the goal of speaking with one voice has seven basic elements.

1. *From the Bottom Up.* Advocates at national, state, and local levels will have to identify all individuals, organizations, and agencies with a stake in arts education generally, and in the specific arts disciplines. This task has largely been accomplished at the national level through the National Coalition for Education in the Arts. Its twenty-seven organizations represent twenty-seven different networks whose members can be activated in support of the Standards. Advocates have to guard, however, against deceiving themselves that activity among the leaders of national organizations constitutes national action. It does not. Advocates at all levels will also have to learn how to surmount the 80/20 rule, that sound principle of organizational life that tells us that in any group, 20 percent of the people do 80 percent of the work. All must be activated to deliver the same message: "The Standards are a good thing because they are good for education and good for kids."

This does not mean that the strategic thrust is from the top down. In fact, the reverse is true; enduring change is almost always generated from the bottom up. As the adage goes, "When the people lead, the leaders will follow." Getting the Standards implemented will happen, if it happens, because decision makers become convinced that the people they decide for want *this* decision.

2. *National Communication.* Advocates, including national organizations, will need to agree on the key messages to be delivered to and by their several constituencies, and will need to make sure these messages are delivered in publications, membership materials, state and local meetings, conferences, and through other vehicles.

3. *Who Benefits?* A large group of potential supporters and advocates—stakeholders, really—can be recruited to support Standards implementation. The quickest way to find out who the stakeholders are is to ask a simple question: "Whose financial well-being is affected—short-term and long-term—by an increase or decrease in the number of students involved in arts education?" The answer to this question will point directly at local businesses, community groups and institutions, civic groups, and others. Just as important, strategically, is enlisting the support of these groups' regional, state, and national networks. In my own industry, which is largely made up of people who turned their love of music into a business career, the logic of this strategy is clear. It applies (with appropriate changes) to theatre, dance, and the visual arts as well:

> The Standards will help improve music education.
>
> What helps music education also helps sell music products.
>
> It is therefore in the financial interest of a local music retailer to support the Standards.
>
> Members of the music-products industry are linked nationally through their own trade association (or other affinity group).

Maximizing individual effectiveness is most readily accomplished by acting together to get the Standards implemented.

This kind of thinking creates a branching pattern that reaches out to a host of allies, including other trade associations, interest groups, and others within the same industry.

4. *Business Support.* Not to be ignored in this process is the business community in general. The most consistent message heard from this segment of society in the last decade has been its deepening concern about the quality and results of American education. Efforts by such organizations as the National Alliance of Business, the National Association of Manufacturers, the Business–Higher Education Forum, and the Business Roundtable have been in no small measure responsible for focusing the debate over education reform. Most encouraging has been the response of business leaders to the message that an education in the arts makes an effective contribution to developing workers with characteristics that businesses need and seek: self-discipline, self-esteem, cooperative work skills, creativity, and imagination. This willingness to respond should be exploited to the maximum in promoting the Standards as a means to those ends.

5. *Choosing Spokespeople.* Arts organizations and identified stakeholders should be encouraged, through their various member networks, to find ways of speaking *together* about their commitment to the Standards. This commitment may take many forms, such as appointing a single spokesperson or group of advocates who can speak for all; working with a public-relations firm or local publicity committees to generate media coverage; generating persuasive arguments on behalf of both arts education and the Standards; and developing a joint print and broadcast media strategy, especially at local levels.

6. *Reaching the Uncommitted.* All arts advocates, organizations, and agencies will need to develop a special communications strategy targeted directly at the unconvinced and the uncommitted. This strategy should include information sessions, publications, conferences, and forums.

7. *A Role for Each Constituency.* Perhaps most important, all members of the arts community who are not yet committed to the Standards will need a clear definition of the specific roles they must each play in an overall advocacy strategy. Too often, good will and energy are dissipated when people don't know what they can do, should do, and are best suited to do.

Issue Two: Creating a Working Constituency

People, more than any other resource, including funds, are what make advocacy effective. The constituency for arts education and for implementing the Standards exists; it simply has yet to be forged into a *working* instrument.

The constituency consists of (a) parents, (b) teachers in both public and private education, (c) school administrators, (d) artists at national, state, and local levels, (e) members of the wider arts community at every level, (f) state and local arts agencies, (g) the business community, (h) higher education, (i) arts students, (j) supporters of local theaters, symphonies, choruses, galleries, and dance groups, including state and local arts alliances, and (k) all those who understand the importance of the arts. As I have noted, the constituency-building task begins with arts organizations and agencies helping their own members find the resources to generate messages that make sense at both state and the grass-roots levels, then working out the implications. In many environments, those messages will focus on the benefits of the Standards and why they have to be implemented.

This will not be an easy task because the content of the Standards, and what they can accomplish, is as yet unknown to many who would become supporters. Many educators at the building level, even arts educators, know little or nothing about the Standards—to say nothing of parents and other potentially sympathetic groups. Without information, these people cannot act. But when they become well enough informed to make an impact on decision makers, they can be sure of being heard. Here, then, is what any advocacy effort will have to tell all those in the groups listed above, if a working constituency is to be formed: "This is what the Standards are. This is what they will deliver to your child and your school. These are the jobs that need to be done. This particular job is your part in getting the Standards implemented. Now go and do it—and report back."

Goal. Forging a working constituency means more than identifying the players, calling the meeting, and crafting the message about what has to be done. It means bringing together not just those who will talk the talk, but those who will walk the walk. In other words, creating a working constituency means handing out jobs; it means giving people something to do and telling them when it has to be done.

Strategies. Developing a working constituency means working in the right direction; this is largely an organizational issue. The organizational task has at least these four dimensions.

1. As noted, effective advocacy support for implementing the Standards must spring from the local level and target its efforts on the immediate and next-higher level of decision making, consonant with Tip O'Neill's sage maxim that "All politics is local." At the building level the target is parents, principals, superintendents, site-based management teams, and school boards. At the school-district level, the target is the board of education, neighboring school districts, the state department of education, and local legislators. At the state level, the target is the state department of education, the governor, and the state legislature.

Advocates will need to bring their networks into play via an enabling strategy rather than a directive one; this is especially true for national arts organizations and agencies. The beginning point is identifying leaders willing and able to start in schools; they need to begin at the level of the table of organization of whatever group those leaders belong to. Cooperation and continuing communication among advocacy groups is essential to facilitate this process and to avoid duplication of labor.

Again, the appropriate analogy for making things happen at the lowest level first comes from the political world. The most important resource in any local political campaign is always shoe leather—not TV time, op-ed pieces, or posters, but people talking to people they know, telling others what's at stake and why it's in their interest to act, and enlisting their support. Those who want to mount an effective advocacy campaign locally will thus have to create the equivalent of leafleting in the shopping malls and ringing doorbells.

2. Once a series of targeted action groups is formed, advocacy organizations can feed them a wide variety of materials suitable for various persuasive and operational tasks. These could range from a leaflet on "How to Persuade a School Board to Adopt the Standards" to a set of talking points on "Why the Arts Standards Are Important to Your Child's Education" to a brochure on "What Site-Based Management Teams Need to Know about the New Arts Standards."

3. Advocacy groups at all levels should take time to establish clear goals for everyone's activity, define objectives, assign tasks, lay down time lines for achieving them, and design some accountability structure for assuring that they are achieved. For example: "Goal: A vote by the school board or site-based management team to adopt the arts Standards as policy."

◆

Forging a working constituency means ... bringing together not just those who will talk the talk, but those who will walk the walk.

◆

A caveat is in order here, however. All seasoned advocates know that nothing can create more damage than a loose cannon. Coordination, therefore, is essential to educate everyone involved in the advocacy effort, to keep everyone's effort on point and moving toward the agreed-upon goals and objectives.

4. Establish horizontal and vertical liaisons with other advocacy groups and networks, share strategies and planning resources, and help one another's advocacy efforts to assure that all are speaking with the same voice.

Issue Three: Developing and Disseminating Advocacy Tools

Just as no candidate ever sent a willing worker into the world without a handful of leaflets and bumper stickers, the working constituency formed to advocate implementation of the arts Standards has to have materials. Fortunately, many of these have already been produced by national arts groups and advocacy organizations that work at the state and local levels.

Making effective use of these materials—and the new ones that will have to be developed—will require an advocacy plan that includes step-by-step goals, check lists, organizing tools (manuals, brochures, phone and fax trees, flyers, tapes), and procedures for their use by local-level advocates. *Planning must be supported and delivered by the four organizations that developed the Standards— the American Alliance for Theatre and Education, the Music Educators National Conference, the National Art Education Association, and the National Dance Association—tapping into their own, one another's, and heretofore uninvolved networks* (for example, PTAs and PTOs, musicians' unions, dance studio teachers, amateur theatre groups, private music teachers, local chambers of commerce, and others).

Included in the materials to be developed should be the following:

1. Materials that make the case—in lay terms—that arts education is basic to all education and not just a frill. Examples abound. In addition to the introductory section of the Standards document itself and *Summary Statement: Education Reform, Standards, and the Arts*, they include such fundamental publications as the National Endowment for the Arts's report, *Toward Civilization*, as well as the host of advocacy materials produced by the organizations that developed the Standards and by the Council for Basic Education. Of value also will be materials developed by organizations formed *specifically* around an advocacy agenda, such as the *Handbook on Advocacy* of the American Arts Alliance and, most recently, the myriad materials produced by the National Coalition for Music Education. Materials developed by state-level arts alliances and projects, such as The Arts in the Basic Curriculum project in South Carolina, can also be very helpful in making the case for arts education.

2. Materials explaining the arts Standards, the rationale for education standards in general, and the impact they are expected to produce.

3. Materials that demonstrate the benefits of arts education in terms that reach beyond their intrinsic value (for example, showing how the arts contribute to self-discipline, the development of higher cognitive skills, group skills, developmental skills, self-esteem, creativity, and the like); as well as the arts' positive impact on such important educational variables as school attendance and dropout rates.

4. Materials laying out the likely consequences of (a) adopting the standards (impact on staff requirements, staff

development, teacher preparation, class scheduling, the school day, assessment issues) and (b) not adopting the standards (further deterioration of arts education, foregone opportunities to integrate diverse curriculum elements, a "cultural caste system," and "right–brain damaged" children).

5. Materials strictly targeted to the mechanics and operations of advocacy—organizing, planning, leadership, and prioritizing.

Goal. Every interested person has a job, knows how to go about it, and knows when it has been completed.

Strategies. Three components of an organizational and dissemination strategy for advocacy materials are important for working in partnerships with the national arts and education organizations who already have state and local networks in place:

1. These organizations are best positioned, and best equipped, to develop and disseminate generic advocacy materials. This is simply inescapable.

2. These organizations can provide technical assistance for advocacy within their own organizational spheres via hot lines and toll-free numbers.

3. Each of these organizations should move now to establish a special liaison function targeted specifically to Standards advocacy and implementation. The individuals assigned this responsibility could work to bring in potential supporters, act as an information clearinghouse within their organization or network, and play matchmaker for those who have the desire to help but

no place to go. In addition, these individuals should form an ad hoc group for sharing information, strategies, and resources across organizations.

Issue Four: Persuading Decision Makers

Finally, the primary focus of all advocacy activity is, of course, decision makers at local and state levels who have the power to adopt and implement the Standards. Every point made about politics at the beginning of this article now reemerges with redoubled force.

Goal. Every decision maker is reached and persuaded that the Standards should be adopted in his or her locale.

Strategies. Four strategies are important to persuading decision makers that implementing the Standards is in their interest and in the interest of the children they serve.

1. Identify every decision maker *and relevant staff person.* This second group is supremely important and often overlooked. Staff are gatekeepers; they often control access to decision makers; they are the "filter" through which decision makers come to an understanding of what people want from them or want them to do. As a general rule, the higher one goes up the decision-making chain, the more important these individuals become. It is crucial to cultivate relationships with staff and make them allies.

2. Contact all decision makers at least once, preferably in a "sit-down" briefing-type session. An opportunity to present your case to a decision maker

one-on-one is precious and cannot be wasted. All such meetings should be *very* carefully prepared for. Ask staff to help you by indicating the decision maker's interests, concerns, and "hot buttons."

3. Make sure every decision maker hears all the arguments. As an advocacy campaign plays itself out, decision makers will align themselves along a spectrum of support for and opposition to implementing the Standards. Even those camped solidly on one or the other end of the spectrum should be kept fully informed; first, because they will not like being written off or taken for granted, and second, because today's opponents quickly become tomorrow's friends (and vice versa). Implementation of the Standards is going to be a long-haul issue; keep in touch.

4. Make sure every decision maker receives materials relevant to decision making, not just the materials that "make the case" for the Standards. Arts advocates tend to believe that their positions on arts issues have intrinsic worth and are self-justifying. Not so. Political people need to know "what's in it for me." Put differently, all politicians want to "do the right thing," but that often involves finding some way to build a bridge between the right thing and the next election. In this sense, in addition to everything else they must be, all advocates have to be bridge builders.

A Final Word of Caution—and Urgency

The implementation of the Standards is necessarily a long-term campaign; it is not a single battle that can be won in one vote taken by a legislature, a resolution passed by a local school board, or the decision of a site-based management team. Teacher preparation and professional development programs will have to change to meet the needs created by these Standards, as will school funding, assessment practices, program-evaluation practices, classroom teaching, and a host of other factors. The results we seek will not be won in a month, a year, perhaps even a decade. The truth is that we cannot lay down the task of implementation until *every* child in *every* school is receiving a balanced, comprehensive, sequential arts education that meets these Standards. All of this means that work cannot begin too soon. And in that regard, I am reminded of a Chinese proverb that tells us, "The best time to plant a tree is twenty years ago. The second-best time is today."

Karl Bruhn recently retired as director of market development for the National Association of Music Merchants, from which position he helped organize the National Coalition for Music Education.

Implementing the National Standards

Developing Professional Resources

Harlan Edward Hoffa

This article will discuss the role of the arts education community in implementing the National Standards for Arts Education, analyze its strengths and weaknesses for that purpose and propose a plan through which its resources may be developed and utilized. The professional community in arts education may be described in several ways, and for some purposes it can include those who teach in social or cultural agencies (such as arts councils, community centers, recreation programs, and professional schools) as well as elementary- and secondary-school teachers of the arts. Because the National Standards refer only to in-school programs, however, an approach to professional development[1] is implied that is limited to K–12 teachers of the visual arts, dance, music, and theatre; to those who hold supervisory or administrative positions in arts education; and to faculty members in colleges and universities who are specifically engaged in the education of such teachers.

Factors Affecting Professional Development

The first and perhaps the most obvious thing to be said about arts education as a concept that spans the visual and performing arts is that it is a fairly recent development whose roots in the academic community are, as yet, quite shallow. Prior to about 1960, the arts were rarely referred to in the collective sense, in education or elsewhere, and even today the term is strangely absent from the Merriam-Webster, Random House, and American Heritage dictionaries.

Among the first to use the term "the arts" in anything like a national forum was President Kennedy, when he appointed August Heckscher as his special consultant on the arts in 1962. That was followed by the creation of the Arts and Humanities Branch in the U.S. Office of Education in 1963 and by passage of the National Arts and Humanities Act two years later, after which the collective noun was commonly used in reference to arts councils or professional associations that had interdisciplinary interests in the arts. In higher education, many of those art, music, theatre, and dance curricula that had previously been administered through the colleges of liberal arts, education, home economics, or physical education coalesced into colleges of the visual and performing árts during that period; at about the same time, a number of state education agencies and school districts redefined their separate art and music supervisory positions in multidisciplinary terms. Several professional journals dealing with education in the arts also came into being in those years, and the four national associations in arts education—the American Alliance for Theatre and Education, the Music Educators National Conference, the National Art Education Association, and the National Dance Association— were drawn into cooperative ventures of several sorts, even as other kinds of arts organizations became active in arts education.

Cooperation between the four national associations has continued to develop, and the *National Arts Education Accord,* published in 1992, is a summary of their shared beliefs. That Accord is also the foundation upon which the Standards were built, and it is a concrete demonstration of the associations' ability to work in concert on issues of common concern. It is equally apparent, however, that there is no such thing as a discipline, a body of content, or a coherent area of study called "arts education"; few, if any, of those who teach art or

music or theatre or dance have abdicated their original disciplines and declared themselves to be generic arts educators instead. And, indeed, the National Standards make no such pretense either because they, too, exist as standards for each of the four disciplines that must be implemented separately though, ideally, in parallel stages. Their most important commonality is that the arts disciplines share a tripartite structure of knowledge consisting of "creating and performing," "perceiving and analyzing," and "understanding cultural and historical contexts" (the conceptual headings under which the writers of the Standards worked out early drafts of the document).

The Strengths and Weaknesses of the Professional Community

Before it is possible to sketch the outlines of a plan for professional development—a plan that is intended to accommodate those new and unique demands that the Standards will impose—several of the arts education community's inherent characteristics, which are so little subject to change that they must be considered immutable, have to be acknowledged as points of departure.

The first given is that the cross-disciplinary term "arts education" first came into general use because a few visionary arts educators, who happened to be in influential positions, worked very hard to promote the idea that all teachers of the arts, regardless of their areas of specialization, would benefit from mutual cooperation instead of competition with each other for increasingly scarce resources. Cooperating also meant that the established hierarchies within each of the disciplines were, of necessity, subordinated to that collaborative effort on occasion, even at some cost to their own autonomy. And it is probably safe to say that such accommodations were not always easy for them to accept. In short, it was not—and is not—an alliance born of inevitability but, rather, one of unvarnished necessity. That fact, as much as any other, will dictate the strategies that bear on professional development in arts education.

When strategic planning is undertaken by a university or a corporation, it is a top-down process emanating from some central authority—a provost or a president, a chief executive officer or a board of directors—with whom responsibility for implementing the resulting plan will then rest. In the absence of any centralized authority or locus of responsibility in arts education, the Standards will almost surely be implemented unevenly and in different time frames from discipline to discipline.

The second of these givens is that the only broadly effective means of communication within and between various parts of the arts education community is through the publications and the convention activities of the four national associations. Even there, it is imperfect, however, because no single publication or professional association that yet exists serves all arts educators equally.

Moreover, art educators rarely pub-lish in music education journals or attend MENC conventions, and the same is true in reverse—partly, one may assume, because they are not often invited and partly because, if invited, they might wonder what they could possibly do or say that would make much sense or any difference in such unfamiliar surroundings. Dance teachers and those who teach theatre are equally isolated from each other, and few, indeed, are the state associations in art or music education that schedule their annual conferences concurrently, that share their mailing lists, or that coordinate their publication programs. Furthermore, because membership in state and national arts education associations is voluntary, those who choose not to sign on and pay their dues, read the publications, or attend conferences are essentially unreachable regardless of what their professional associations may do. As imperfect as those associations might be, and as unpredictably as their priorities may shift from one election of officers to the next, they provide the only channels of communication that now exist within the arts education community.

The third reality in arts education is that the authority for determining the shape of instructional content in the arts, as well as how those who teach them are to be prepared, rests with state education agencies and, in a carrot-or-stick world, they hold the stick. If, perchance, all fifty of the states were to adopt the Standards as the basis for what should be taught in the arts and then proceed to adapt their requirements for teacher credentials[2] accordingly, the necessary changes in professional training would be a done deal; under such circumstances, teacher training institutions would have little choice but to change their programs in response to those new demands that state education agencies would then have mandated.

◆

The associations ... are the nexus of arts education and the clearest voice for its beliefs and values.

◆

Such an eventuality is remote to say the least, however, so the last of these immutables in arts education is the influence that accrediting agencies exercise in determining the content of instruction and, indirectly, on the scope of professional training as well. The criteria that such agencies apply do not have the force of law behind them, but, even so, they are probably more amenable to those changes that the Standards will entail than are fifty state education agencies whose bureaucratic—and perhaps political—processes may be ponderous, stifling to change, and incapable of coordinated action. Moreover, the criteria that accrediting agencies apply when they exercise their

judgments are based almost exclusively on professional considerations rather than on those extrinsic factors that may apply in a political milieu.

But how, then, are those changes in professional training that the Standards mandate to be communicated to the accrediting agencies and state education agencies whose influence is so inescapable? For that, it is necessary to return once again to the four national associations and, in so doing, to complete a circle of influence brokers that is composed, first, of state education agencies; second, of accrediting agencies; and, third, of the professional associations; all of whom must share star billing in any professional development plan. Among those, however, it is the associations that are the nexus of arts education and the clearest voice for its beliefs and values.

The Plan

The goals of professional development in this frame of reference are first—and of utmost importance—to marshal support for the concept of national standards within the arts education community; second, to institute reviews of pre-service and in-service programs[3] through which arts teachers are prepared, in order to determine whether they are consistent with the Standards and, if necessary, to suggest any changes that may be required; third, to recommend appropriate credentialing requirements for teachers of the arts to assure that teachers have all of the performance/production skills,

cultural/historical knowledge, and ana-
lytical/perceptual abilities that the
Standards will require; fourth, to propose that national and regional accrediting organizations incorporate the triform
of arts knowledge upon which the
Standards are based as part of their
evaluative criteria; and, fifth, to develop
adequate instructional resources in concert with changes in teacher education.

Selling the Idea Internally

The very idea of establishing uniform
and unvarying standards for "what every
young American should know and be
able to do in the arts" is foreign to most
arts teachers, and to some, it may be
anathema as well. Teachers of the arts—
probably more than those of other subjects, where studying the work of tower-
ing genius is less dominant and where
the cult of creative freedom is less
ingrained—are subject to what the
Pulitzer Prize–winning playwright, Tony
Kuschner, has called the "myth of the
individual." Such a myth, like most, car-
ries more than a grain of truth within it;
therefore, regardless of what else is
done, any attempt to implement the
Standards will be futile unless the arts
education community supports it from
within its own ranks. The past several
decades have seen more than a few
instances of exemplary programs in arts
education that have been highly effective
locally but which have produced few significant changes in how the arts are
taught nationwide. These have included
CEMREL's Aesthetic Education Program,
the Impact Project, the JDR 3d Fund's

Art in Education Program, the Getty
Center for Education in the Arts, and
several others, all of which were highly
successful as lighthouse projects and as
demonstrations of excellence. In the long
run, and in spite of their localized successes, they proved to be anomalies
rather than harbingers of revolutionary
change, partly because they depended
upon an infusion of external resources,
and partly because teachers tended to
view them as something special that
existed in a world far removed from their
workaday existence.

The lesson of those exemplary programs—which most teachers admired
but which few could hope to emulate—is
that it will take the entire community of
arts educators acting in concert, rather
than the exemplary excellence of a few
demonstration projects, to implement
the Standards nationwide. Thus far,
however, the idea of national standards
is so unfamiliar to most arts teachers
that its pros and cons have not yet been
debated at any national forum, nor have
questions about their effects on jealously
guarded academic and artistic freedoms
been addressed. The need, therefore, is
for a marketing campaign in behalf of
the Standards, which is aimed at those
teachers who must, in the final analysis,
implement them in their own classrooms. The responsibility for such an
effort—which would, in fact, be much
like a political campaign, complete with
briefing books, sound bites, talking
points, photo ops, and all the rest—probably has to be borne by the four national
associations for two almost inescapable

reasons: first, because it was through their parenting efforts that the National Standards were conceived, fostered, and nurtured in the first place and, second, because the associations are the only channels through which arts educators can speak to one another on issues of substance. The vehicles for such communication are their ongoing publications, the voices of their elected officers, and their annual convention programs, all of which lend themselves admirably to such an undertaking.

The first recommendation of this paper is, therefore, that the four national associations—individually or, preferably, in concert with each other—designate a share of their publications, their officers' travel accounts, and their convention programs to selling the concept of national standards—as well as the reality of the National Standards for Arts Education—to their members. Such a commitment by those associations might, at a minimum, involve at least two articles per year in the regularly published journals of each association for at least three years, two major sessions at each of their annual conventions during that same period, and putting their national officers on the road to address the issue of national standards before as many of their state association meetings as possible.

In addition, the four associations should seriously consider a jointly sponsored two- or three-day conference, the main purpose of which would be to bring arts educators and school administrators up to speed on the Standards. A second objective of such a conference would be to demonstrate the feasibility of interdisciplinary professional meetings in arts education—meetings that have thus far been most notable by their absence. The proposed conference could be self-supporting through registration and exhibitor fees, though its planning and development will probably demand a significant commitment of association resources at the outset.

Selling the Idea Externally

As important as internal variables in the arts education community might be in implementing the Standards, those factors that bear upon it from the outside are scarcely less so and, here too, it falls to the national associations to become the professional image-meisters. An article in *The New York Times Magazine* (October 31, 1993) that dealt with spin doctors on the national political scene noted that "What is really important [about a political issue or figure] is the perceived image." Much the same sort of conclusion could probably be drawn about the primacy of image over reality in television advertising, about the merits of an Ivy League education, about owning an ugly watchdog, about affairs of the heart where love is demonstrably blind, and about matters of art where beauty is said to exist solely in the eye of the beholder. For better or worse, controlling what is perceived to be real regarding arts education may, therefore, be as important as sustaining its more objective reality—and perhaps even more so for some purposes.

For those reasons, this article's second recommendation is that the Consortium of National Arts Education Associations underwrite a coordinated, well-structured, and sophisticated campaign not merely to polish arts education's image but, in fact, to remake that image where necessary. Such a campaign should be specifically directed toward securing support for the Standards from those outside the immediate arts education community, up to and including those in the broadly defined world of the arts, some of whom—like the parable about four blind men who try to describe an elephant—tend to define the whole of arts education as only that part within their grasp. The second audience for such a campaign, and one which has more clout—though perhaps a less vocal interest in arts education—are organizations representing decision makers in the world of schools and schooling: administrators and educational policy makers. The primary purpose of such a campaign should be to assure that virtues of the arts in education are presented convincingly and consistently to all of those whose influence or authority affects its course and its well-being regardless of circumstance or occasion.

Teaching Credentials

For all practical purposes, the only legally binding constraints on any part of arts education are the credentialing requirements that state education agencies mandate. Once credentialed, however, teachers of the arts are free to construct their own curricula, to choose their own instructional materials and, in general, to conduct their classes pretty much as they wish. In fact, in the absence of consistently used texts and other instructional signposts or much in the way of agreed-upon educational goals, teachers of the arts have had few choices but to go their own ways. Moreover, school administrators are equally at liberty to exercise their own priorities and values when allocating the resources that are available to them—which may or may not result in full recognition of the needs of the arts. Not surprisingly, such a laissez-faire system has resulted in great disparity between what is taught in the name of the arts from one district to another and even from one school to another within the same district.

When implemented, the National Standards for Arts Education promise to narrow the gap between the best and the worst of what happens in arts education by providing a consistent set of guidelines for all concerned—teachers, administrators, and policymakers alike. Even so, they will lack the force of law unless the requirements for teacher credentials are changed to assure that those who teach the arts, regardless of whether they are arts specialists or elementary classroom generalists, have the preparation that is necessary to conduct their classes according to the guidelines laid down by the National Standards and unless some effort is made to ensure that school administrators understand something of that triform of knowledge that the arts embody.

The third recommendation is, therefore, that each of the fifty-six state or district education agencies reassess their credentialing requirements for teachers of art, music, theatre, and dance to assure that those upon whom they set their stamp of approval will be prepared to conduct their classes in accordance with the Standards. The broad outlines of what that preparation might be were indirectly (but not intentionally) suggested by the Army's Chief of Staff in an interview in *American Heritage* magazine (December 1993). General Sullivan remarked that his ideal officer would be like Dave Brubeck: classically trained, but also a highly skilled improvisationist. He might equally well have mentioned Wynton Marsalis or Jackson Pollock or Mikhail Baryshnikov, all of whom share Brubeck's classical background and improvisational skills, and in each of whom arts educators might also find an eminently suitable model of excellence.

The credentialing of teachers of dance and theatre as separate specializations should also be instituted where it does not now exist. Comparable attention should be paid to the arts in the credentialing of elementary classroom teachers and principals because they, not arts specialists, will often be responsible for implementing the Standards at those grade levels. The Council of Chief State School Officers is in a uniquely advantageous position to coordinate such an assessment and to assure a measure of consistency from state to state, assuming, of course, that the orga-

nization is willing to commit its resources to the task.

Preservice Teacher Training

As previously noted, the preservice training of teachers of the arts is, of necessity, tied to the requirements for a state teaching credential. Therefore, if those state-mandated requirements for a teaching credential are changed to attain a better balance between the traditions of the conservatory or the atelier, which now prevail, and those of the library and the lecture hall, which the Standards will require, colleges and universities must alter their programs accordingly. Beyond that, the accreditation agencies for such programs—the National Council for the Accreditation of Teacher Education and constituent organizations in the National Office for Arts Accreditation in Higher Education (National Association of Schools of Art and Design, National Association of Schools of Dance, National Association of Schools of Music, and National Association of Schools of Theatre)—also have the clout to assure that teachers will be prepared to implement the National Standards in their classrooms. The immediate problem that such an effort will likely face is the need for greater program depth in arts history and arts criticism than currently exists—and, unfortunately, there is little room in most curricula for additional requirements except at the expense of something already there. One solution to that problem would be to reduce the number of performance or studio courses that are now required and to substitute lecture courses in history and criticism. Such a proposal would be deeply divisive on some campuses, however, thus leaving arts educators caught between the irresistible force of changing credential requirements and the immovable object of entrenched artist-teacher traditions.

A second possibility would be to consider a five-year program of preservice teacher training in the arts such as that which exists in some Scandinavian countries. Such a program ought not be merely the rehashing of a four-year studio or performance degree with a fifth year of pedagogy tacked on at the end, however. It should, instead, be a totally integrated five-year curriculum that is geared to preparing arts teachers for the challenge of implementing a new and different kind of arts education in the nation's schools. Such a step would, admittedly, be loaded with problems, not the least of which are the additional tuition and instructional costs that would be involved, the scarcity of courses in arts criticism that the "perceiving and analyzing" aspects of the National Standards would require (lit-crit courses are more commonly offered), and the glacial pace of all curricular change in higher education.

A third option to the preservice training conundrum would be a two-track system in which some students would follow the traditional performance/production path, while others would choose to concentrate on arts history, criticism, and aesthetics instead and be credentialed accordingly. Such programs now exist in related areas (museum education, for example) though they are, admittedly, uncommon. Teachers of English seem to have solved a similar problem in the teaching of literature on one hand and teaching creative writing on the other; their example may provide useful lessons to teachers of the visual and the performing arts as well. In any event, a typical BA or BS degree comprising 120–130 credits should require no less than sixty credits of course work in the appropriate arts discipline (which is roughly comparable to most BAs but less than is required for a BFA degree) divided one-third/two-thirds, either way, between performance/production and arts history and criticism.

In-Service Training

A certain amount of consistency can be expected among undergraduate teachers-in-training. Most will be young, few will have had much real-world work experience, and their ideals will be more intact than at any time thereafter. None of that can be said with certainty about in-service teachers, however, and the landscape of in-service training is more diffuse as a result. Such training may involve academic degree programs—master's degrees for arts teachers and doctorates for arts supervisors and teacher educators—or fellowships such as those that are occasionally offered through the National Endowment for the Humanities, which focus on the history, theory and criticism of the arts—or institutes and workshops provided by local school systems and professional associations—or, last but not least, independent study.

The periodic recredentialing of teachers is not usually required but, if implemented, would clearly serve to upgrade and maintain the command of subject matter that excellent teaching requires. Such recertification, though uncommon in education, is routinely required of physicians and other professionals and, if implemented, might also serve to revitalize those teacher-oriented summer programs at colleges and universities that have fallen on hard times due to low enrollments and high costs. The responsibility for recredentialing would, of course, fall to state education agencies, and it would have to apply equally to all teachers, not just those in the arts. It would, therefore, become an issue that teachers' unions would surely insist on considering and, when that happened, it would inevitably have implications for school boards, taxpayer groups, and legislators, regardless of the advantages that might accrue to teachers and their students.

It is obviously difficult, if not impossible, to isolate mandated in-service professional development for arts teachers from what would be required of other teachers. Fewer such inhibitions exist with in-service training opportunities that are optional, however, and this article's recommendations will therefore focus on such programs, most of which must, of necessity, result from effective lobbying by the four national associations in arts education. The first of these recommendations, though scarcely necessary, is to urge those associations to continue to work with the two Endowments and with the U. S. Department of Education in order to secure fellowships for teachers of the arts that are comparable in scope, quantity, and variety to those that are offered to science and math teachers through the National Science Foundation.

The second such recommendation is for the associations to provide aid, counsel, and support to state education agencies and to national accreditation groups in an effort to make their in-service requirements more systematic and more rigorous. The corollary of such a recommendation is that those agencies and organizations should rely upon the four arts education associations as their primary source for such assistance.

Third, the national associations should work toward establishing collaborative agreements with colleges and universities to provide academic credit for selected preconference institutes and workshops for arts teachers by utilizing the resources that regional arts agencies and universities may afford. As in the past—and in the immediately foreseeable future—the burden of most in-service training will inevitably be borne by individual teachers on their own time and at their own expense.

Material Resources

Earlier in this paper, "professional development" was defined almost exclusively in people terms, though with the caveat that it was not necessarily limited to the education of teachers and administrators. And, indeed, no such definition would be complete without mentioning the development of instructional resources as well. The supplies, spaces, and equipment that most schools provide for arts instruction are based on preconceptions about the kind of activities that must be accommodated. Traditionally, these have included studio and exhibition facilities for the visual arts; and performance, rehearsal, and practice spaces for the performing arts; plus adequate storage areas and the necessary utilities, on the assumption that what goes on in arts classrooms is modeled on the hands-on ways that artists work, rather than the reading, looking, and listening modes of arts scholarship. Because the Standards will require facilities for both kinds of instruction, resources of an entirely different order must now be provided, as must additional audiovisual hardware and software and expanded library holdings. The publishers of such material have increased their offerings considerably in recent years, but the synergy between teaching materials in the arts and those who do the teaching remains far from perfect (though a useful model for the development of new instructional materials might be found in science education, where the lab and the library have always been considered equally important).

In any event, the economic burden of providing instructional resources for a new kind of arts education must probably be borne by already hard-pressed school systems, while that of developing such materials remains with the pub-lishers and other suppliers who must provide materials of sufficient interest and variety to meet the needs of teachers. Market conditions will probably determine much of what those publishers and manufacturers produce, but it also falls to the national and state associations to apply their own professional standards when they assess the content of advertisements in their journals and the quality of products that are displayed in commercial exhibits at their conventions. Wherever possible, the associations should also advise their commercial suppliers regarding changes on the professional scene that may affect the marketability of their existing products, and alert them to opportunities for the development of new materials when they are needed.

Summary

Professional development aimed at implementing the National Standards is, of necessity, a complex and multidimensional process that involves the national organizations in arts education, state education agencies, accrediting agencies, teacher education programs in the arts at colleges and universities, and perhaps the two National Endowments and the U.S. Department of Education. Key players in that group are the national associations and state education agencies: the first, because they alone maintain an information network that can connect all teachers of the arts to each other, and the second, because they establish the qualifications for those who will be legally empowered to teach the arts.

The most immediate need in professional development—and by all accounts the most essential—is to convince teachers that the concept of national standards for arts education is both feasible and desirable. Without their willing participation, little classroom change will take place, regardless of what others may do or whatever may happen elsewhere. Teachers are, indeed, the key to implementing the National Standards in the only places they will ever count for much—the classrooms, rehearsal halls, studios, and auditoriums of the nation's schools.

Notes

1. "Professional development" includes, but is not limited to, the preservice and in-service education of teachers of art, music, theatre, and dance, as well as that training that is required of elementary classroom teachers when they are called upon to teach the arts in the absence of specialists. It also refers to the preparation of educational leaders whose decision-making authority impinges upon arts education—educational administrators and arts supervisors—plus those faculty members or administrators in higher education whose responsibilities include the preparation of teachers of the arts.

2. "Teaching credential" is used in this context rather than "teaching certificate" or "teaching license" even though the three terms are often used interchangeably. It indicates that the holder has met the requirements of a state education agency to teach a specific subject, such as English or mathematics, or to teach at designated grade levels, broadly prescribed in most instances as elementary or secondary. Art and music teachers are usually credentialed to teach K–12. Theatre and dance teachers may be credentialed in other disciplines such as English, speech, or physical education, especially where state education agencies do not issue teaching credentials in those arts disciplines.

3. "Preservice" refers to those aspects of preprofessional training that are controlled by undergraduate degree requirements and by teacher credentialing standards. Preservice training in arts education is usually a full-time program of study that leads to a baccalaureate degree and a teaching credential in one of the arts. "In-service" refers to that training that is undertaken after a teacher has entered the professional workplace.

Harlan Edward Hoffa is professor emeritus of art education and associate dean emeritus (research and graduate studies) in the College of Arts and Architecture at The Pennsylvania State University in State College.

unities in the
om

Perspective

mpolla

ement stan-
National
ion are com-
hey establish
bring quality
n's schools.
They recognize that all students, including those with disabilities, those at risk, and the gifted and talented, deserve access to the knowledge and experiences that the arts provide. But if they are left only in written form, the Standards will have little impact on children or classrooms. To do what they have the potential to do, they must be implemented.

One response to the challenge of implementing the Standards for students is the parallel effort to define standards for schools and teachers as well. It is, after all, unfair to expect students to achieve specified levels of knowledge and skill if they lack access to the opportunities and resources (whether curricula, staff, facilities, or materials) to attain them. Sometimes called "opportunity-to-learn standards," these criteria would define the resources necessary for a school to offer children the best chance to attain the levels set forth for the various academic areas, including those in the National Standards for Arts Education.

In the arts, resources are particularly important, since dance, music, theatre, and the visual arts have traditionally been relegated to a secondary status in our schools. If teachers or school systems are to be held accountable for student attainment of the Standards, the necessary tools must be provided. But this raises a further question: Are negative consequences generated by a focus on tangible resources alone? Are not the *intangible* resources of commitment, will, and the perseverance of those who believe in the value of comprehensive and rigorous arts programs just as vital to implementing the Standards? The issue of intangible resources is particularly important because across the nation the current delivery of the arts curriculum is decentralized, subject to state and local prerogatives. All the academic standards are voluntary; their authority is moral, not legal.

Because the Standards are voluntary, students' opportunities for attaining them are often wildly uneven. Both economic inequity and the effect of dispersed decision making are manifested in the availability and quality of staff, materials, and facilities. These factors make an impact on learning opportunities. Competition for scarce resources is the norm, and arts programs frequently lose. Too often, the arts are forced to compete with one another for the same scarce budget line, and even for the same students.

While developing arts education standards that establish a fundamental body of knowledge and skill is important as a first step, it will not alleviate the problems of inequity, nor will the Standards, by their existence alone, help students achieve. Ideally, local advocacy efforts would inform educational policymakers on all levels of the richness and value possible in adopting the arts Standards. In the best of all possible worlds, ample and equitable resources would flow naturally from informing decision makers of the need for support, thus ensuring implementation across the nation. But in the real world, implementing the Standards will require tremendous effort and time.

Two Scenarios

◆ In the fall, Miss Gardener, an elementary school music teacher, began to augment her curriculum and lessons by introducing her students to diverse styles of music and their cultural contexts. She had the students sing songs from their own ethnic traditions in each class, after which she discussed some of the songs' unusual images and ideas and teaches students some of the history of the songs. This winter, the traditional concert will draw on these multicultural experiences. Her principal has reminded her how important parental support is for the music program and has commended her for the changes she has introduced. The music budget for next year—always tight—is in its formative stages, and Miss Gardener believes that the concert she has planned will promote the music program more effectively in the community, which is ethnically, racially, and culturally diverse.

◆ Brett, a senior, elected his first high school art course to help fill his schedule. He declared an interest in art and has shown some talent for it; part of his motivation was the memory of having enjoyed an eighth-grade art class. But within the first few weeks of the semester, he begins voicing his discontent. The class discussions, the homework, and reflective writing are not what he had anticipated. "What happened to regular art?" he asks his guidance counselor. "If I had wanted another academic course, I would have signed up for biology. It would have looked better on my transcript." His guidance counselor writes this note on his petition to withdraw: "Brett enjoys art but doesn't enjoy the class. Credits are not needed to graduate. Transfer approved."

Here are two schools, one in which richer content is supported by an administrator who understands and values the unique learning possible through the arts and the kind of community relations that arts programs can generate; the other a school in which a teacher must contend with a system in which arts programs are optional, vulnerable to student whim, and viewed as somehow "not academic." The constraints on implementing higher standards are as obvious as they are disheartening. How do arts teachers successfully address opportunities to learn when instructional time with students is insufficient and classes are overcrowded? How do teachers make good instructional decisions without the time to plan and exchange information and ideas with their colleagues? How do arts teachers teach to the new Standards with inadequate staff training or professional development?

Teachers of English, mathematics, and other core subjects will undoubtedly be challenged by the high levels delineated in their own content and achievement standards, but arts teachers may face the greatest challenge of all. The place of traditional academic subjects in the curriculum is, after all, established. Whether the arts Standards are high or low, a student is still required to pass a requisite number of English, mathematics, and other courses to graduate from high school. Even in the twenty-nine states where there is an arts requirement for graduation, it is often minimal or may be replaced by an elective. The nation's continuing concern about our

ability to compete scientifically and technologically is reflected in the substantial taxpayer support given to science and mathematics education through the National Science Foundation and other sources external to the local schools. Arts programs need this same type of investment.

If existing arts programs are to be sustained and to grow, then arts educators must, like Miss Gardener, be creatively responsive to student needs, aware of local resources, and in tune with school and community expectations. The arts educator, with direct pupil contact, can also offer valuable insight into what works best in the classroom.

Policy decisions on state and local levels about implementing the arts Standards and securing opportunities to meet them must also be influenced by the arts teacher's unique perspective. If implementation of the National Standards for Arts Education puts the arts in competition with other subject areas for scarce resources locally, that is because the historical pattern has been that the success of one area comes at the expense of another. If that tradition holds, as is likely, the arts will continue to suffer more than other academic areas. Advocacy efforts and implementation strategies must be crafted with this zero-sum game in mind; otherwise, the opportunity to learn in the arts will continue to be reduced rather than enhanced. If old patterns are to be replaced, a top-to-bottom reordering of instructional and support priorities is required.

Opportunity-to-Learn Means Changing the System

The issue of opportunities to learn will be addressed successfully only when school systems consider the constraints imposed by current values and practices and develop the long-range plans needed for reform. The Standards are part of an overall shift in that direction; what they now need is momentum. But momentum will not come simply by demanding more from an already overburdened system. Only a multidimensional transformation of our schools can provide excellence in opportunity as well as excellence in instruction. Currently, for example, there is a general failure to address diverse learning styles. Our schools often do not meet the needs of at-risk students, disaffected students, students from dysfunctional families, and gifted students. Only when the entire school has a shared vision, in which all members of the school community (students, parents, teachers, administrators) have a stake, can the capacity and capabilities for renewal be developed. It is in that environment that the Standards can be implemented most successfully and that the opportunity to learn can become the norm.

The Standards encourage a variety of methods, resources, and experiences to enhance learning. Both by nature and by adaptive responses to their environments, arts educators are innovative, resourceful, and creative in their teaching. The real impediments to greater substantive learning are found more often in the system within which they work than in a lack of material resources. Thus, systemic reform is necessary if the Standards are to pervade classroom instruction. Several components of this broad-based change are particularly important.

Professional Development. Staff development for teachers should be continuous and should highlight the unique contributions of the arts as both process and content. Considering the complex nature of teaching and the time and energy it requires, an inability to stay informed of research or a time lag in embracing new ideas is understandable. Cooperative learning, teaching to diverse learning styles and populations, site-based management, effective discipline, writing across the curriculum, basic skills, and authentic assessment are only a few of the topics competing for the attention of classroom teachers and administrators. Under these circumstances, it is likely that, despite national media coverage, many arts educators, principals, and other administrators are still unaware, or only vaguely aware, of the Standards.

Staff development provides the chance to educate teachers across the curriculum about the value of arts education, both as process and as content. Further, implementing the Standards will require training for classroom teachers, counselors, and administrators. For arts educators trained primarily in European traditions, for example, teaching students to understand and analyze works of art from outside these traditions may prove a daunting challenge. It is imperative that the openness of the Standards to a multicultural perspective in the arts not be undercut by stereotypes, unintentional tokenism, or the use of inappropriate terminology (for example, "primitive").

Students' opportunities to learn cannot be maximized unless they are accompanied by continuing opportunities for teachers to grow professionally. These staff-development opportunities should not be limited to course work, workshops, or summer institutes. In-service training and classroom support should be an integral part of the staff-development program in every district and school. Additionally, the timing of staff development within the school day, week, and year must be carefully planned to maximize its effectiveness and underscore its importance.

Increased Awareness of the Value of the Standards. State and local education policymakers, school board members, and community leaders provide philosophical and financial support for programs through staff, resources, and materials—all of which are imperative to the future of arts education programs. It is most important that these decision makers learn the value of arts education. Developing this awareness might be accomplished through the continued advocacy efforts of the arts and education communities. A state report card that reflects the efforts of local districts and schools, for example, could provide an incentive for local policy makers to acquire this awareness and act on it.

Time for Teachers to Grow. Maximiz-

ing the opportunities for student learning is contingent on the time teachers have to plan that learning. Thus, time must be built into the daily schedule for teachers to interact and exchange ideas. An instructive difference between professional development for teachers in Japan and those in the United States is that in Japan, teachers rarely teach all day. Their schedules normally contain two to four hours that are expected to be used for collaborative lesson planning, personal study, and sharing ideas and information with their colleagues.

◆

Staff development for teachers should be continuous and should highlight the unique contributions of the arts as both process and content.

◆

Teachers with the time to interact in this way are empowered; they learn more about teaching their subjects and their students. While the Standards maintain the integrity of each arts discipline, they also recognize the importance of connections within the arts and between the arts and other school subjects; it is important that teachers have the time to

foster such connections and relationships.

Time to Teach. The usual organizational structure of American schools
fragments the school day. Elementary
students adhere to a rigid daily schedule
within a single classroom, while high
school students typically change subjects, locations, and teachers every forty-
five minutes. This traditional approach
to scheduling must be challenged
because it impedes opportunities to
learn within the arts, imposing an artifi-
cial time frame on activities that does
not support the learning needs of students.

◆

*Implementing the
Standards is an exciting
challenge to those in the
arts community
nationwide who have
participated in their
development.*

◆

*Acknowledging Diverse Learning
Styles.* Content that engages students is
essential to providing opportunities to
learn in the arts. Those who create arts
curricula must consider students' interests, motivations, and cultural contexts
if these are to have meaning for students

as individuals. Teaching this content
also requires being responsive to diverse
learning styles to maximize achievement.

The needs of all students, including
students at risk, disaffected students,
students from dysfunctional families,
and gifted students, must be addressed
through in-class support, social programs, and appropriate resources,
including technology. Stimulating environments within and outside the school
should include taking advantage of nontraditional opportunities to enhance
learning, such as theaters, arts centers,
studios, museums, and galleries. A field
trip is a viable means of connecting the
school experience to the outside world,
relating the arts to one another and to
other subjects, and developing dynamic
interactions between subject areas not
previously reinforced. By itself, exposure
to these extraschool environments is not
enough to develop culturally literate students—but it is necessary.

Authentic Assessment. School systems that implement the Standards
must evaluate their continuing effectiveness, in terms of both student learning
and the responsiveness of the school
system to student needs. The system
must at all costs remain vital and capable of self-renewal.

Assessing students' performances
and portfolios is essential for learning in
the arts. Fortunately, arts educators are
skilled in using these measures, which
have only recently been introduced to
other content areas. These and other
forms of assessment, including written
responses and observations by practi-

tioners, should be developed to measure classroom and studio learning.

Also, fortunately, the Standards are being implemented at the same time as the National Assessment of Educational Progress (NAEP) in the arts, scheduled for 1996. This timing enables the two efforts to be consistent and mutually supportive. Their coming together now can direct national attention toward what students know and can do in the arts, identify differences and inequities related to achievement, and help teachers and administrators learn what works. This information will be useful for developing curricula and programs in which all students have the opportunity to learn and to reach high levels of achievement.

An Exciting Challenge. Implementing the Standards is an exciting challenge to those in the arts community nationwide

who have participated in their development. It is encouraging to note the addition of the arts to the Goals 2000: Educate America Act, which places the arts squarely in the core curriculum. The richness of the Standards and this support by our government should compel the education community to reflect on the place of the arts in our schools, on how the arts are taught, and on the kind of school environment the arts need if they are to flourish. Such reflection is a first step in the process of systemic educational reform that is needed to implement the Standards and to provide all students with an opportunity to experience the power of the arts for learning and for life.

Barbara Fehrs-Rampolla teaches visual art in the Holmdel (New Jersey) Schools.

Making Disciplinary Connections

Samuel Hope

Introduction and Overview

There is a tendency in American practice to find a productive concept, overpromise about it, overpromote it, then discard it because it did not live up to its billing. When it becomes obvious that a positive spin can be created by using a term, pervasive and indiscriminate exploitation often follows. Our nation's policy discussions thus seem to center around one panacea at a time. Certain panaceas seem to arrive periodically, perhaps fulfilling some mysterious cycle. As the National Standards for Arts Education are being published, it seems that "interdisciplinary" is the latest manifestation of this syndrome.

Clearly, interdisciplinary studies and capabilities are too important to be trivialized. They represent only one of many approaches to combining disciplines. Avoiding bandwagon superficialities is critical now, because the world and its technologies are becoming more complex. A changing world calls for real capabilities within, across, and among disciplines. Achieving and maintaining these capabilities means substantive work, not hype, bumper-sticker analysis, or knee-jerk responses.

We need to recognize that combining the disciplines is intrinsically neither good nor bad, and that gains or losses from combining disciplines are anything but guaranteed. As is true for almost everything else in education, success depends on the integrity of ends, and on the ability to build effective synergies between ends and means. Thus, the most productive efforts on the question of combining disciplines will be found not in promoting particular pros or cons, nor in appropriating popular terms for partisan purposes, but in careful thought.

The best place to start is with what students need to know and be able to do about relationships between wholes and parts at specific points in their education. Although there is no standard answer for all students, there are specific answers involving the arts for specific groups of students in specific locations at specific times. This article reviews the issues that need to be thought through as teachers and those who support them make decisions about purpose, content, and method in arts education.

Disciplines in General. The sum total of human knowledge and skills can be considered as one giant, ever-expanding universe. But the whole also has parts. Various constellations of knowledge and skills gather around unique perspectives and modes of thought. For centuries, human beings have argued over ways to name, describe, separate, and reflect the interdependence of these perspectives and modes. One result of that effort is the several academic disciplines, each with its own knowledge, skills, and intellectual approaches. Consider a ball that rolls across a table and bounces on the floor. Physics and history each will tell us something quite different about such an event, while in a work of art, the ball and table will be used to produce a particular effect. The physicist or historian can tell us in great detail what happened, while the artist makes such an event meaningful in the context of a specific work.

The intellectual world is full of disciplines, subdisciplines, and disciplinary combinations simply because there are so many ways to look at things. To continue our analogy, however, if students are to understand balls rolling off tables or anything else from a particular scientific, historical, artistic, or other perspective, they must first acquire the knowledge and skills necessary to work from

those perspectives. Their work can be simple or complex—a stopwatch measurement or a ballistic calculation. The one requires only the ability to work with numbers, the other an understanding of the laws of physics. But all ability is built on previously acquired abilities. The mind cannot work with nothing.

Obviously, a student can enjoy watching balls roll off a table without going further. But self-satisfaction is not education in the sense represented by the National Standards in the various academic disciplines. Education requires effort to gain deeper understanding. The more competence a student gains in the various disciplines, the more knowledge, skills, and perspectives that student can bring to any problem, issue, or event. That is why thoughtful educators through the centuries have fashioned curricula that provide developing minds with access to several ways of thinking, knowing, and doing, as represented by the arts, humanities, and sciences. The national movement that has produced voluntary, K–12 Standards continues this long tradition.

The Arts Disciplines Specifically. In terms of the basic approaches they take, the sciences try to find out what things are and how they work, history tries to describe what happened, and philosophy addresses the question of what things mean. The approach of the arts is to make new things, or to make things new. These four functions are all present to some degree in all endeavors that involve the intellect. Basic work in any discipline usually focuses on gaining competence in its most central aspects. A child beginning mathematics focuses on learning how to add, not on the history, philosophy, or aesthetic pleasures of computation. In fact, some mastery of basic mathematics is necessary before these other perspectives can be addressed in any depth. Dance, music, theatre, and the visual arts are no different; each has its own starting point and fundamentals. The arts Standards present goals for core knowledge and skill development in each of these four disciplines, recognizing the differences among them.

For each arts discipline, the Standards promote both work *in* the art form and work *about* it. Work *in* the art form means making new things or making things new. Work *about* the art form involves learning how the art form works and what happened in its development; it also involves exploring what the art form and its body of works mean in various contexts. The ability to do work *about* an art form supports the ability to work *in* it, and vice versa. The Standards recognize and promote this interdependence by bringing the intellectual functions of art, science, history, and philosophy together with the knowledge, skills, subject matters, and purposes of dance, music, theatre, and the visual arts. In this sense, study of each arts discipline is intrinsically interdisciplinary.

Because the several arts disciplines represent different ways of making new things or making things new, the Standards consider them separately. Obviously, music and dance are not the same even though they often appear together; the same applies to theatre and the visual arts. Each has powers the other lacks. Each molds content and intellectual functions from all disciplines and from life itself, shaping them by using its own specific media and techniques. These facts provide the rationale for separate study. Indeed, there is no such discipline as "the arts." Each art form offers a different way of thinking and knowing, or in one well-known formulation, is derived from a different "frame of mind."[1] The arts are one in the same sense that all knowledge is one, but as we have seen, this truth is not particularly useful in developing the range of competencies students need to become broadly educated. Substantive pursuit of each art form uses various intelligences and disciplines, but as we have also seen, this truth must be used to create discipline-focused capabilities of substance and depth. To do otherwise is to deny students the most profound benefits of arts education.

◆

For each arts discipline, the Standards promote both work in *the art form and work* about *it.*

◆

Combining Disciplines. The arts Standards deal with parts of the whole by denoting specific aspects of work *in* and work *about* a specific art form. Capabilities with parts enable capabilities with wholes. This truth has a broader application. The more capabilities a student acquires with the individual arts, humanities, and sciences, the more capabilities he or she has to combine them in meaningful ways. Yet the ability to integrate work in two or more disciplines is not the only worthwhile goal; indeed, each combination of disciplines stems from its own purposes and produces its own results. The first implementation question, therefore, is not *how* but *what*. What purpose is being pursued? What are the goals for learning?

At the simple end of the spectrum, the teacher's objective might be to use terms associated with one discipline in teaching another. Students learning to count can count notes, paintings, or actors in costume as well as any other object. While such uses are to be encouraged, to ask students to count pairs of ballet shoes does not teach them dance. At the other end of the spectrum are efforts that require an in-depth mastery of the disciplines to be combined—a project on classicism in the arts and politics of the eighteenth century, for example.

If students are to gain optimum benefits, educators who would combine disciplines at the K–12 level must be clear about their purposes, and fashion their choices, expectations, approaches—and public relations—accordingly. It is too easy to produce mere symbols of a discipline without developing its knowledge and skills. Learning songs by rote for a

school musical is not the same thing as learning music as a discipline. Both are worthwhile, but each serves a different purpose: one culminates in a single event, the other opens the door to the intellectual realm encompassed by the art of music. The same principle applies to purposes for all forms of combination. To repeat, the first implementation question is, What are the purposes? Once that question is answered with integrity, specific approaches and methods can follow.

Another implementation question involves the politics and funding of K–12 education. Professionals in the disciplines and subdisciplines are often characterized as special interest groups unconcerned about the whole. Sometimes these characterizations are fair, sometimes not. But special interests, agendas, and power issues are everywhere. To the extent that K–12 education focuses on gaining and combining disciplinary competence, leadership must come from those with competence in the disciplines involved. Yet such individuals regularly lose their strategic influence when the educational priority becomes simply using the facts and vocabularies of one discipline to teach another, or combining subject matters in superficial ways to produce the image, but not the substance, of interdisciplinary study. And, because the relative power of various groups' agendas influences decisions about funding, the issue of disciplines in combination is always more than a pure search for wisdom about the best interests of students. The

Standards statements, focused as they are on content, provide an important means of creating and evaluating proposals for combining disciplines on the basis of what students are expected to learn, not who has control.

Issues for Implementation

Integrity. Because the universe of knowledge and skills is already so vast, curriculum builders always exclude more than they include as they decide what is most important for specific students at a particular time. K–12 education is often and perhaps best thought of as the period when students acquire a foundation of basic knowledge and skills—that is, functional competence— that provides access to virtually any discipline. But integrity in building that foundation begins with being honest about the selective nature of making curricular choices: students are always gaining one thing at the expense of another. Integrity also means honesty about the need, at times, to sacrifice breadth for depth and vice versa. Exercising integrity is difficult in a period when so many people think of every moment as an advertising moment and nothing more, an approach regularly encountered in calls for arts education to concentrate on specific kinds of art, arts professions, uses of art, causes, personalities, or historical periods, rather than on the fundamentals of work *in* and *about* the disciplines themselves.

These considerations and conditions become particularly acute when decisions are being made to combine studies across the arts or to bring the arts into relationships with other disciplines. Integrity means ensuring that programs combining disciplines are honest about how they advance the knowledge and skills of students. What, for example, will students gain or lose by a given decision about content, method, or use of time? Integrity also means careful use of language, not using fancy buzzwords to indicate simple objectives. For example, many of the ways disciplines are brought together are not "interdisciplinary" at all, and calling them that is ultimately counterproductive and confusing. When concerned educators find a new word in the interest of precision, the result is often a rolling barrage that destroys language and meaning as it skews the focus on critical functions of education. Ultimately, no one wins, and students lose most.

Educational Goals and Objectives. There is an infinite number of possibilities for combining the subject matters, modes of thought, techniques, and philosophies of various disciplines. Beyond simple applications that use vocabularies, symbols, or the subject matter of one discipline to teach another, there are two basic approaches:

♦ *Process Focus.* This emphasizes experience with techniques. Knowledge and skills in at least two subject-matter areas are used to demonstrate multiple dimensions, or at more advanced levels, to teach methods for combining disciplines. Here, content serves technique.

♦ *Content Focus.* This emphasizes

searches for new insights or information, or produces new products by using combinations of knowledge and skills to achieve specific purposes. Here, technique serves content.

Each of these two basic approaches may address and involve various types and levels of integration. Several common approaches are:

♦ *Disciplinary*—refers to a specific body of teachable knowledge with its own background of education, training, procedures, methods, and content areas. Example: dance or mathematics or history.

♦ *Multidisciplinary*—refers to the juxtaposition of various disciplines, sometimes with no apparent connection among them. Example: theatre plus mathematics plus history.

♦ *Pluridisciplinary*—refers to bringing together disciplines assumed to be more or less related. Example: mathematics plus physics, or French plus Latin plus Greek, which constituted the "classical humanities" in France.

♦ *Cross-disciplinary*—refers to imposing the fundamental principles of one discipline on another discipline. Example: the structural forms of music are used as organizing principles in literature.

♦ *Interdisciplinary*—refers to the *interaction* among two or more different disciplines. This interaction may range from simple communication of ideas to the mutual integration of organizing concepts, methods, procedures, and the like. Example: studying the relationship

between scientific and artistic ideas in a structure such as the Eiffel Tower.

♦ *Transdisciplinary*—refers to establishing a common system of axioms for a set of disciplines. Example: anthropology considered as "the science of human beings and their accomplishments, including the arts."[2]

Neither using elements of one discipline to teach another, nor the process or content focus, nor the descriptors listed above are the only ways of thinking about disciplines in combination. But by combining these concepts and the arts education Standards, teachers have an extensive palette from which to create specific objectives and compile corresponding curricula, units, or lesson plans that address two or more disciplines in a substantive way.

Content and Methods. Content and methods should exhibit a logical relationship to educational goals and objectives. If true disciplinary integration is desired, for example, the necessary conditions must be in place, the first of which are the prerequisites for student participation. What knowledge and skills must students bring if they are to work substantively in a particular curriculum, lesson, or project? The assumption that credibility comes automatically with promising to do the most complex things at the earliest age almost guarantees that they will be done superficially. But in many circumstances, simple juxtapositions of the disciplines can be appropriate, sufficient, and productive. Whatever the level, educators must give careful thought to the relationships between wholes and parts, and they must do so in a way that does not pretend that providing an experience develops competence. For those teaching the arts disciplines, efforts with more than one discipline involve decisions about:

- which portions of the Standards will be addressed;
- the content and methods associated with portions chosen;
- the goals, content, and methods necessary for the proposed combination; and
- the approaches and evaluations necessary to ensure the desired relationships between wholes and parts.

Factors Affecting Success. Teachers cannot structure, teach, or evaluate things that they do not know or cannot do themselves. Most people, whether teachers or not, must work hard to master one disciplinary perspective in great depth. However, almost everyone can master the fundamentals of several subject-matter areas. This fact encourages work within and across disciplines. But if success in combining disciplines is to be ours, the first resource is competent, capable teachers. The second is similar. Students must acquire enough knowledge and skills to ensure some success when reaching beyond their current abilities and skills. Other resources, such as time, technology, funding, will, and commitment are all important, but no amount of them will obviate the need for student and teacher competence.

The time needed for learning obviously varies with the student and the task. The arts Standards provide a way to use achievement goals for specific content to predict and control how much time is needed. Normally, teachers will need extra time to prepare curricula and lessons that involve more than one discipline. If time is not available to think deeply, plan carefully, and teach patiently, serious doubts arise about the substance and depth of learning that will occur when disciplines are combined.

Will and commitment are affected by the disciplinary organization of academic and intellectual life, especially beyond high school. Since time is limited, students have little incentive to devote themselves extensively to work at combining disciplines when their futures are tied to demonstrations of high-level performance in specific disciplines. Although these conditions may change, this reality necessarily exerts a major influence on planning and implementation.

Can technology help with time, will, and commitment? Yes and no. Technology can provide instant access to a vast range of subject matter. It can speed compilation and presentation. It can demonstrate a range of possibilities quickly and graphically. All these are useful, but they cannot replace individual competence in setting goals and achieving them by choosing effectively from the array of possibilities. Thus, technological capability means little without the competence to use it effectively. Moreover, it will take time, will, and commitment for students to achieve even a basic command of technological tools and resources. Nonetheless, technological skills can facilitate pursuit of the intellectual techniques of the process focus, or the intellectual goals of the content focus.

Evaluation. Productive evaluation is based on a clear understanding of goals and objectives and the roles of content, methods, and resources in achieving them. The more specific the expectations, the more specific evaluation can be. If, for example, students are expected to understand that the arts disciplines can be mutually reinforcing, evaluation might consist of seeking students' reactions to the various elements in a particular staged or filmed work. If, however, students are seeking an in-depth understanding of how various ideas underlying the arts disciplines are related to one another in a certain historical period, then an evaluation of their understanding must be based to some extent on their demonstration of knowledge and skill in those arts disciplines, the methods of correlation and integration being used, and the general history and philosophy of the era being studied. There are countless other examples, but there is one fundamental principle for arts educators: evaluate the arts aspect of combined disciplinary efforts against applicable portions of the arts Standards. To what extent are students learning to work *in* or *about* one or more art forms in the combined effort? How do these achievements compare with original goals? The whole range of evaluation

methods can be brought to this task.

Public Relations. As this analysis has shown, using disciplines in combination is complex—full of promise if used wisely. Students are more important than bandwagons, basics more important than fashion, content more important than labels. Public-relations efforts to promote the Standards should reflect these priorities. Public-relations techniques can cover lack of substance only so long. If the concept of "disciplines in combination" or the term "interdisciplinary" are used carelessly, and if educators are not honest about expectations and achievements, both will eventually be discredited. Opportunities to help students become increasingly sophisticated about how parts and wholes are related will be lost—at least for a time.

◆

If time is not available to think deeply, plan carefully, and teach patiently, serious doubts arise about the substance and depth of learning that will occur when disciplines are combined.

◆

It is particularly important to avoid creating the false impression that any combination of disciplines will automatically produce competence in all disciplines, or that programs focused on combinations are inherently more valuable than those focused on individual disciplines. Within a school, curriculum, course, or lesson, changes back and forth from one focus to the other should be happening regularly in pursuit of comprehensive education. The Standards provide content-based means for demonstrating that the arts are academically substantive, just as the standards for the other K–12 disciplines provide the same resource for those disciplines.

Parts and Wholes

As the total universe of knowledge and skills continues to expand, it seems increasingly important to develop students' capabilities for bringing multiple perspectives to any issue, event, question, or enterprise. Since all knowledge is linked, it is possible to start anywhere and make connections with everything else. Yet, wherever one wishes to start, focus is essential.

Implementing the K–12 arts education Standards when disciplines are combined means keeping various possibilities in perspective and, at best, using each of them to enhance competence in dance, music, theatre, and the visual arts. Disciplinary competence in each enables students to bring their unique perspectives to bear on the universe of knowledge and skills. It does not matter very much whether a teacher starts with parts or wholes, as long as he or she

works within, across, and among the disciplines to help students gain the competence to move back and forth between them.

Perhaps the most critical thing is to avoid creating the impression, either for students or for ourselves, that consideration of the whole can substitute for competence in the parts, or that competence in the parts obviates the need for working with the whole. As is the case in most things in education, success comes to those who are able to create appropriate mixtures and balances, leading students to specific competencies and overall comprehension at the same time. The overarching question of implementation is how to do this best, keeping content and process in a productive relationship, and remembering that education is a lifelong process that deserves the firmest of foundations in the K–12 years.

Notes

1. See Howard Gardner, *Frames of Mind: The Theory of Multiple Intelligences*. New York: Basic Books, 1983.

2. These definitions are paraphrased from *Interdisciplinarity: Problems of Teaching and Research in Universities*, Organization for Economic Cooperation and Development, 1972, pages 25–26. They are widely accepted by those concerned with various levels of integration and academic programs.

Samuel Hope is executive director of the National Office for Arts Accreditation in Higher Education and an executive editor of *Arts Education Policy Review* magazine.

Issues of Assessment

Paul R. Lehman

The Challenge

The establishment of national, voluntary content and achievement standards for K–12 arts education represents only one step in the current effort to develop a world-class education system for America's students. The most difficult task will be to find sufficient resources to implement the Standards. But there's another challenge that is almost equally difficult: creating an array of effective strategies to assess student achievement in the arts.

Assessment in the arts is a complex task, fraught with problems and pitfalls, although it will unquestionably become a major force in American education in the near future. The Goals 2000: Educate America Act charges the National Education Standards and Improvement Council (NESIC) not only with certifying "voluntary national content and student performance standards that define what American students should know and be able to do," but also with certifying "systems of assessments submitted by States on a voluntary basis, if they are aligned with State content standards certified by the Council [which] are valid, reliable, and fair when used for their intended purposes."

It's difficult to assess problem-solving ability and higher-order thinking skills. It's difficult to write guidelines for scoring students' dance improvisations, dramatic scripts, or musical compositions. It's difficult to define a task that measures imagination or creativity. But it can be done.

The challenge in each of the arts is to develop models of how to assess students' success in meeting the National Standards for Arts Education. What is called for is a catalog of strategies and techniques for identifying student achievement in each individual standard. The catalog should include techniques that can be used—by teachers, schools, and states—for all the various purposes for which assessment is undertaken.

The national voluntary content and achievement standards in the arts set forth expectations about what American students should know and be able to do on exiting grades four, eight, and twelve. Some of the achievement standards in the arts tend to be much less specific

◆

To discuss assessment meaningfully, one must specify the context.

◆

than others. The intent is to allow for varying interpretations within acceptable, defined limits. Varying interpretations require varying assessment tasks, however. Since several assessment tasks may provide relevant information concerning the same achievement standard, there can be no one instrument for assessing nationally whether the standards have been met in any of the arts.

Purposes and Contexts of Assessment

There are many reasons why assessment is important and useful in any discipline. For example, assessment can:

◆ inform students, parents, and teachers of progress toward meeting objectives and standards;
◆ demonstrate to students and parents the types of learning and levels of achievement sought by the school;

◆ aid the instructional process by providing the teacher with data on the effectiveness of instruction;
◆ motivate student learning; and
◆ provide information to policymakers at all levels to aid in decision making.

To discuss assessment meaningfully, one must specify the context. There are many settings in which learning in the arts is assessed. When an ensemble performs in rehearsal, or when a student offers a comment, the teacher typically makes an assessment. That kind of informal assessment takes place continuously in the classroom. It's such an integral part of the instructional process that neither teacher nor student thinks of the teacher's reaction as assessment, but it is.

Teachers also assess their students' work in more structured ways over longer periods, ranging from a few days to several weeks. Most teachers must assign grades to students every few weeks and every term. Students assess their own work and that of their peers. Schools try to assess their instructional programs so as to report to the community on their effectiveness. External funding agencies seek to gauge the effectiveness of programs they have funded. States, increasingly, are creating programs of systematic assessment to compare student performance over time. And the National Assessment of Educational Progress (NAEP) is gaining increased visibility by doing the same thing at the national level.

But one cannot use the same

assessment techniques in all these contexts. Thus, discussions of techniques should be linked to clear statements of the purposes of the assessment. Some assessment techniques are useful in more situations than others, but there is no single assessment technique and no general-purpose formula for assessment that will solve all the assessment problems arts teachers face.

Categories of Arts Assessment

The skills and knowledge set forth in the arts Standards tend to fall into three categories: (1) creating, (2) performing, and (3) responding to works of art. In the first two categories, particularly, artists and arts educators have a long tradition of assessment. Music compositions, plays, and works of art are judged in competitions of every sort at every level on a regular basis. They are also evaluated informally by listeners and viewers whenever they are performed or displayed. Different evaluators may reach different conclusions, however, because they come from different backgrounds and apply different criteria. In educational assessment, a way must be found to ensure consistency (the technical term is reliability) so that, insofar as possible, the results of a given assessment are the same no matter who does the assessment or when or where it is done. Achieving reliability constitutes a major, continuing challenge in performance-based assessment.

Performance competitions, similarly, are commonplace in the world of the arts. There are any number of competitions for professional artists, especially in music. Newspaper critics assess performances daily. Tens of thousands of elementary and secondary school students participate in competitions in the performing arts each year. Student works are regularly judged in poster and drawing competitions, and performances of dance, music, and theatre are held in schools across the nation, where it is expected that listeners and viewers will evaluate the results.

Responding to works of art includes analyzing, describing, and evaluating. It includes understanding relationships among the arts and between the arts and other disciplines. It involves understanding the arts in relation to history and culture. There are fewer precedents, however, in assessing responses to works of art than in assessing creation and performance. This is due, in part, to the widespread view that responding to art is an individual matter—that there are no right answers. A few standardized tests in music and visual arts were published, beginning in the 1920s. They tested factual knowledge, often in a multiple-choice format, but none achieved anything approaching the widespread acceptance of comparable tests in reading and mathematics.

Assessment Techniques

In most cases, portfolio assessment (a portfolio is a collection of samples of a student's work over time) will be the most useful strategy for assessing students' creative work in the arts. The earliest successful uses of portfolios in large-scale assessment were in the Advanced Placement examination in studio art and in the National Assessment of Educational Progress in art, both dating from the early 1970s. Currently, portfolio assessment is being used with particular effectiveness in the Arts PROPEL project in the Pittsburgh schools.

Portfolio assessment is particularly important in the visual arts, but is useful in the other arts as well. Not only can a portfolio contain a student's music compositions or play scripts; it can also contain audiotapes of music improvisations and videotapes of performances in dance or theatre. A portfolio can document the creative work, the performances, and the responses of the student over an extended period. It can include the notes, sketches, and products that demonstrate growth over time.

Although portfolio assessment is a useful technique, it is not in itself a solution to the problems of assessment. Once the materials are assembled, they must still be assessed reliably according to established criteria.

The most important principle to consider is that arts assessment must be authentic. That is, the assessment technique used must be consistent with the nature of the skill or knowledge. If the task is to play the piano or to dance, the assessment strategy must be based on a sample of the student playing the piano or dancing. If the task is to create a work of art within specified guidelines, the assessment strategy must be based on a work of art created by the student. Even the assessment of knowledge should be

based on how the knowledge is applied in real-life situations. This requires that the student perform some task beyond marking a response in a multiple-choice test. In the current jargon, the assessment must be performance-based.

Performance-based assessment has a specialized meaning in the arts, as well as a general meaning. Teachers in other disciplines are just now discovering it, but arts educators have used performance-based assessment for generations. Indeed, there is no category of assessment in which arts educators have more experience than in performance. Professionals in all of the performing arts audition for positions regularly. Student musicians audition for "chairs" in every band and orchestra. Juried competitions in the visual arts, while not often school-based, are nonetheless common. Competitions in the arts do not produce "objective" scores, as in basketball or baseball, but they can produce scores based on judgments, as in figure skating or diving.

The district and state music competitions, for example, in which thousands of large and small ensembles and soloists participate every year, offer one useful precedent for large-scale assessment in the performing arts. These elementary and secondary students are typically judged according to criteria outlined on a judging sheet. Large ensembles are normally evaluated by three judges to achieve greater reliability. Even so, there is no research to document the reliability of these assessments over time and across geographical areas, and it is likely that serious discrepancies exist.

One requirement in any systematic assessment effort is a clear understanding of the desired outcome. That requirement is satisfied by the arts achievement standards. The next step is to translate the outcome into performance tasks that can be assessed reliably. Reliability requires that the essential characteristics of an acceptable response must be identified and the criteria for scoring must be established. Typically, the scoring is done by one of two methods, holistic or incremental, depending on the nature of the task. In holistic scoring, usually three to five sets of descriptions or characteristics of achievement—sometimes called benchmarks—are used, and the student's response is assessed on the basis of which level his or her performance most closely approximates. In incremental scoring, a certain number of points is assigned for each desired element of the response, and the total number of points represents the individual's score.

Assessment has traditionally been norm-based; that is, a student's score indicates where he or she ranks in relation to a specified group. Increasingly, however, current assessment is criterion-based. This means that the result for each individual indicates only whether he or she met a particular criterion or set of criteria. In the case of assessment based on national voluntary achievement standards, it is probably sufficient for most purposes to know whether the students have achieved the standard, although the National Assessment of Educational Progress rec-

ognizes three levels: basic, proficient, and advanced.

◆

One requirement in any systematic assessment effort is a clear understanding of the desired outcome.

◆

Two advantages of criterion-based assessment are that it decreases the likelihood of excessive competition among students and is more consistent with the goals of cooperative learning. It is especially important that students not fear assessment but use it both as a way to learn and as a way to measure their own progress.

Useful Precedents

The most successful precedent for large-scale performance assessment in the performing arts is probably the music portion of the National Assessment of Educational Progress (NAEP), conducted in 1971–72, in which students were required to perform, sight-read, improvise, and create music. These exercises were scored with a high degree of reliability. Significantly, performance was eliminated from the NAEP music assessment in 1978–79 because of the expense involved. Fortunately, all four of the arts are scheduled to be included in an authentic, performance-based NAEP assessment in 1996. The strategies planned for the 1996 assessment will likely provide especially useful models for assessment in the arts.

The best current models of large-scale assessment in responding to works of art may be found in the Advanced Placement (AP) examinations in music and the visual arts administered from the early 1970s through the present. These examinations are developed by committees of the College Board and administered by the Educational Testing Service (ETS). Essay and short-response items have been included in the AP exams from the earliest years. Reliable scoring has been achieved by means of systematic and thorough training of scorers and by frequent spot checks.

In recent years the Graduate Record Examination in Music, also administered by ETS, has included a variety of respondent-constructed items. These have used a variety of formats, some of which have required minimal training of scorers. Another ETS program, the National Teacher Examination (NTE) in Music, has included only multiple-choice items until the present; but in accordance with the requirements of the new PRAXIS series of exams that are replacing the NTE, a committee is currently at work developing a variety of respondent-constructed items. It is likely that the strategies being devised will provide additional useful models for assessment in all the arts.

Limits and Caveats

Assessment in the arts is receiving considerable attention these days, but the results are mixed. In one state, for example, arts educators were encouraged when the arts were included in the statewide assessment plan. Unfortunately, the state has discovered that, because of the number of students involved and the projected costs, it will probably be necessary to limit their assessment to multiple-choice, machine-scored items. It is inevitable that any assessment exercise that must be scored individually, such as a performance, is more expensive than one that can be scored by machine; relatively few useful items in the arts (such as knowledge of specific information) can be machine-scored.

Fortunately, the limitations of strictly machine-scoreable assessment are being recognized in other disciplines as well. The AP program includes respondent-constructed exercises in all disciplines, including math, physics, and chemistry. Several state assessment programs, notably in Vermont, include pioneering efforts to use performance-based assessment. The models being developed in the humanistic disciplines in these programs will likely be useful for arts educators as well. In addition, we can learn from the arts assessment efforts being piloted in Australia and the Netherlands.

Given the nature of the arts, some degree of judgment will always be needed in assessing whether students have met a given standard. For this reason, achieving reliability will always be a challenge. The solution is to define and describe, with as much precision as possible, the evidence that will demonstrate that the standard has been met. It is not easy to establish precisely a dividing line in such a way that any achievement above the line is acceptable and any achievement below it is not. But that is what standards are all about. The task is difficult but achievable. What is important is that the line be established thoughtfully and with care.

Can we envision newspaper headlines reporting that eighth-graders' scores in reading and math have dropped slightly during the past three years, but that their scores in theatre and dance are up? Or that minority twelfth graders in the East and Midwest have made major gains in science while their scores in the visual arts are unchanged? Or that 76 percent of fourth graders in Japan can sight-sing at the proficient level while only 43 percent can in the U.S., but by the twelfth grade the U.S. has narrowed the gap to 65 percent in Japan versus 59 percent in the U.S.?

Many arts educators would likely find such reporting repugnant, while others believe that these data are precisely what are needed, because nothing less dramatic can capture the attention of the public. Whatever one's opinion, there seem to be indications on every hand that comparative data such as these reflect the forces that are driving American education. It is important that the American public retain its perspective by remembering that the purpose of education should be the pursuit of truth and beauty, the development of human

capacities, and the improvement of the quality of life. And there is nothing that can be taught in school that contributes more to these purposes than the arts.

What Lies Ahead?

In the coming years, NAEP will likely achieve greater visibility and will be looked to increasingly as a model of assessment practices. It is timely that the arts are being included in NAEP once again, and the types of arts assessment exercises being designed for NAEP will provide useful models for arts assessment at all levels. Not every type of assessment exercise useful in the classroom is useful in NAEP, by any means, but every type of assessment exercise useful in NAEP will be useful in the classroom.

The relationship between NAEP and state assessment programs is still evolving. Some states want NAEP results to be made available at the state level, which would require an increase in the NAEP sample size and thus an increase in cost. Whether state-level NAEP results are made available or not, NAEP could share unreleased items for use in state assessments. Released items can be used for comparison purposes by anyone at any level.

The arts should be a part of any school-wide or district-wide assessment program undertaken. In the classroom itself there will be more emphasis on continuing assessment than on end-of-unit assessment, while assessment strategies used at the school or district level may be based on those used at the national or state level. Additional exercises appropriate to the local setting should also be developed, since many of the constraints concerning vocabulary, methodology, and equipment that limit item-writers at the national level do not exist at the local level. In any event, unique local features characteristic of the arts programs in the community should be reflected in the assessment strategies used.

During the next few years, we should see the focus shift away from standardized tests toward individualized assessment of student progress, based on explicit standards for student achievement as expressed in state frameworks. National standards may be adopted intact by states or districts, but more often they are likely to serve as a basis for adaptation.

In the coming years, the major action will take place in state capitals and in the classroom. States will continue to need help in developing their assessment systems in the arts. They will also need to distinguish between the information that is most useful for improving instruction and that which is merely easiest to test. They will need to learn how to avoid the abuses of assessment, and they will need to learn the most cost-effective procedures.

Arts educators will need help in meeting the assessment requirements of education reform as it applies in the classroom. They will need help from school districts, state education agencies, and professional associations in the form of conferences, seminars, and publications. Their assessment efforts should extend to themselves and their programs as well as to their students. In particular, they need help in developing more formal assessment techniques and in assessing problem-solving ability and higher-order thinking skills.

There is a powerful reservoir of support for arts education existing in the various constituencies represented in this publication. The difficult task ahead is to figure out how to mobilize that support to get the Standards adopted and implemented at the state and local levels, and how to utilize the Standards to improve student learning. The effective assessment of student achievement will be essential in this effort.

Paul R. Lehman is professor and senior associate dean of the School of Music at the University of Michigan, Ann Arbor. He served as chair of the Music Standards Task Force for the National Standards for Arts Education.

A Nuts-and-Bolts Plan for Parents

Kitty Waikart

Parents are naturally concerned about the quality of education available to their children. They want each child to receive the best possible preparation for a healthy, happy, productive, and successful life. That includes being able to participate in, appreciate, and enjoy the arts.

Parents know what research confirms—that by studying the arts their children can develop important skills in problem solving, critical thinking, teamwork, and self-discipline. Many parents have also seen that quality arts programs help schools address issues such as at-risk students, readiness, and dropout prevention. When asked to reflect on what needs to happen for our schools to achieve the excellence demanded by the twenty-first century, parents are thus quick to conclude that the curriculum must include substantive arts education. Fortunately, the National Standards for Arts Education are able to provide direction in moving toward excellence in arts education.

It is important, therefore, for parents to understand what the Standards are and what they seek to accomplish. In simplest terms, they are statements of what children should know and be able to do in the arts in grades K–12. They are not an arts curriculum handed down from Washington. They leave the means—the educational methods and theory—to local schools, school districts, and teachers. By their support for the Standards, parents show that they are convinced that the competencies outlined there are worth developing.

But, to make a difference, the Standards must be implemented, and parents should be part of that process. But what does it mean to insist on parental involvement? Simply that parents have a vital role to play because their concerns are focused on the arena of implementation, the classrooms where their own children spend day after day.

PTA

This paper provides nuts-and-bolts strategies for parents to use to help implement the Standards. The best way to begin is through parent support groups in local schools. The National Congress of Parents and Teachers (PTA) can help. The PTA is organized into individual local units, fifty state units, plus Europe, the Pacific, and Washington, D.C.; all PTA members make up the National PTA. The PTA's commitment to the arts led to its fine arts program, "Reflections," which began in 1968–69. In 1992–93, student participation reached more than 600,000.

In 1979, the PTA affirmed the arts as "essential elements" in school curricula across the nation. Until the current Standards were developed, however, PTAs had no guidelines for their efforts to improve local arts education. Through the years, the PTA has also developed and distributed a variety of programs, materials, and kits designed to increase parental awareness of the importance of quality arts education and to train them as advocates (see Appendix A for selected resources).

This article offers a set of sequential strategies for parents to follow in working for Standards implementation: assessing the school situation, assessing the community situation, and coalition building.

Step One: Assessing the School Situation

The first strategic step, as with any campaign, is to get the lay of the land by assessing the arts program in the local school. The results of the assessment should be a report, which can serve as

the basis for an action campaign. If the school has a PTA, its Cultural Arts/Reflections Committee is the appropriate group to undertake the assessment. The PTA kit, *School Is What WE Make It! A Parent Involvement Planning Kit*, guides parents through the process of evaluating all kinds of school programs; it is readily adaptable to arts programming.

If there is no PTA, any parent or group of parents can form a committee and conduct the evaluation. Throughout the assessment process, one of the easiest jobs is also one of the most important: making lists. Committee members should compile and regularly update a list of names, addresses, and phone numbers of all individuals and groups who will help with efforts to implement the Standards. These names and numbers should be converted into a telephone tree, a basic organizational tool.

On the substantive side, assessing the arts program means reading and becoming thoroughly familiar with the Standards. When looking at the curriculum, the basic question parents should ask is: "Where is the arts education program now, and what changes must be made to meet the Standards?" For example, the curriculum should provide all children with a balanced, comprehensive, sequential, substantive, and rigorous program of instruction in all four of the arts disciplines—dance, music, theatre, and the visual arts. If it doesn't, parents can take steps to get these areas included.

Certification. The next area to assess

is the quality of instruction; teacher certification is a key to this. Are all arts classes taught by teachers certified in the arts areas? If not, inquire about district and state policies governing employment of arts teachers. A majority of states have certification requirements for music and visual arts teachers, but only a few certify teachers for dance and theatre. Sometimes, even after certification requirements are in place, problems finding qualified teachers persist, particularly in rural or isolated areas. Sometimes communities and schools need time to develop and attract the necessary staff and resources. But regardless of the problems, parents must insist that schools provide qualified teachers to prepare students to meet the Standards in all the arts.

Time. The time allotted in the school day for arts classes is another area to assess. In most states where the arts are included in the curriculum, elementary schools provide a block of time for the arts per day or per week. At the secondary level, however, the arts curriculum may not be what it appears to be. A school may offer a broad range of courses in the arts without providing time for students to take them. Consequently, not all students may be able to fit arts courses in their schedules. For example, the only class for members of the jazz ensemble may be offered during the same period as a competing mathematics class that figures prominently into college entrance requirements. Any student interested in both would have to choose.

Interdisciplinary Classes and Extra Opportunities. All classes should have an interdisciplinary dimension. For example, history teachers should include material on how the arts affected the period of history the class is studying. As a follow-up on this issue, the assessment should see whether state schools and departments of education require students majoring in education to take classes in the arts and in methods for integrating the arts with other disciplines. If not, the committee should inquire about how to add these skills to existing teacher-education courses.

◆

Parents must insist that schools provide qualified teachers to prepare students to meet the Standards in all the arts.

◆

Students also need opportunities to attend art exhibits and live theatre, concerts, and dance performances, as well as opportunities to demonstrate their accomplishments in the arts by their own performances and exhibits. School "career days" should include information on careers in the arts, presented by professionals. "Artist-in-residence" programs give students a chance to see, hear, and interact with professional artists and should be available to all students in the school.

The Report. When the assessment of the school arts program is completed, the report should enumerate the arts programs currently available and provide an evaluation of their quality, based on the competencies outlined in the Standards. For example, the report should address who is teaching the arts programs and what qualifications and standards they had to meet in order to teach in the arts.

If the school has a PTA, the report should be presented to the PTA board with a recommendation that the members adopt a resolution to address the inadequacies in the school arts program. The committee should have the resolution ready and present it to the board.

Copies of the resolution along with the report should be given to the principal and the curriculum administrator for the school. Copies of the resolution and the assessment report should also be sent to the state PTA Resolutions Committee and the state PTA president, along with a request that the state PTA Resolutions Committee consider the issues addressed and offer a similar resolution to delegates at the state convention. Offer to help gather additional information if any is needed.

If the school does not have a PTA, the committee should give copies of the report to the principal and the curriculum administrator. In either case, after allowing sufficient time for study of the report, the committee should meet with administrators to discuss how its objectives can be met. Barriers, such as time, other curriculum mandates, funding,

---

A Resolution on Arts Programming

Whereas: The arts are basic to education; and

Whereas: The National Standards for Arts Education are nationally promulgated and endorsed guidelines for what children should know and be able to do in the arts in grades K–4, grades 5–8, and grades 9–12; and

Whereas: The Thomas Jefferson Elementary School lacks essential elements to assure the implementation of these Standards, be it therefore

Resolved: That the Thomas Jefferson Elementary School PTA create a public awareness of the importance of quality arts education; and be it further

Resolved: That the Thomas Jefferson Elementary School PTA advocate improved arts education programs in the Hometown, Pennsylvania, School District to help students achieve the competencies outlined in *National Standards for Arts Education;* and be it further

Resolved: That the Thomas Jefferson Elementary School PTA advocate the implementation of the National Standards for Arts Education in all schools in the district.

Adopted on this _____ day of _____, 199_, at the regularly stated meeting of the Thomas Jefferson Elementary School PTA.

availability of qualified teachers, and availability of resources to implement the Standards, should be openly discussed with sensitivity to the limitations of school officials and budgets.

If implementing the Standards at the school level is not within the authority of school building officials (this will probably be the case), the next step is to approach the school board and the superintendent. Since delegates from one school probably will not carry enough weight to influence the district policymakers to make significant changes, parents in other district schools can be enlisted and helped to evaluate their schools' programs. To further strengthen the case, parents can assess community resources and form an arts education coalition with the community to help implement the Standards.

Step Two: Assessing the Community's Cultural Assets

It is important for parents to focus on what local arts councils, professional organizations, individual artists, and arts educators are doing to promote the Standards in the community and in the schools. If no organized efforts are currently under way, ask for help from the community in promoting the Standards and in making the changes needed for local school programs to meet them. If the arts community is promoting the Standards, try to find ways to bolster one another's efforts. *Performing Together: The Arts and Education* is a joint publication of the American

Association of School Administrators and the Alliance for Arts Education that provides specific questions parents need to answer in assessing the arts resources of the community.

Find out, for example, what groups offer artist-in-residence programs. Are they paid for by the local school, the PTA, the school district, the state? Is the funding equitable? That is, are programs available to all schools for nominal costs, or are they only available to schools with significant financial resources? What is the quality of these programs? How do they help students develop the competencies indicated in the Standards? What additional activities and individuals can local arts groups make available to students to increase the knowledge and skills outlined in the Standards?

In addition to assessing the community's resources in the arts, make an assessment of what educational opportunities in the arts are sponsored by local civic, fraternal, or religious organizations. Local businesses may manufacture or merchandise arts-related products; local music stores may offer lessons. Institutions of higher education frequently offer opportunities for arts study and cultural enrichment to high school students. Are any of these groups engaged in activities to support the Standards? If not, solicit their input and assistance.

The committee should compile all information gathered on the community's resources into a report paralleling the school assessment report. The report should discuss what resources the community has and how they can be used to meet the Standards.

Armed with the school and community reports, parents will have the persuasive information they need to influence decision makers. To be effective, all the individuals and groups should speak with one voice, gathering momentum and strength as they pull together all the players necessary to make changes and implement the Standards.

Step Three: Form an Arts Education Coalition

When the reports have been completed, arts advocacy kits such as *Be Smart, Include Art* (developed by the National PTA and the J. Paul Getty Endowment) and the *Action Kit for Music Education* (developed by the National Coalition for Music Education), will be useful for the next step: coalition building. The purpose of any coalition is to organize an alliance of groups with a common goal. If a coalition is already working to meet the Standards, check into how parents can become an active part of the group. The PTA "Nuts and Bolts" guide, *Coalitions: Joining Them, Building Them, and Making Them Work,* is an excellent source.

The first step in organizing the coalition is for the parents' committee to discuss which individuals or groups should belong. It is important to make the base as broad as possible, because bringing diverse groups together adds credibility and depth. Groups invited to join should include, but not be limited to, the following:

- local school teachers and administrators
- parents from other schools in the district
- school district administrators
- school board members
- local arts alliances
- professional associations in the arts
- education associations
- arts educators and arts administrators in higher education
- representatives from educational television and radio
- business leaders (particularly anyone whose business is to manufacture or merchandise arts or arts education materials)
- the local chamber of commerce (they usually have an education committee)
- local and state politicians (especially those on education or arts/cultural affairs committees)
- religious leaders (music or choir directors)
- leaders in senior citizen groups
- the arts curriculum coordinator from the state department of education
- all persons and groups identified in the school and community assessments as interested in arts education

With the participants identified, the committee chairperson should write to several of the above groups with a proposal and a date for an organizational meeting. When the groups agree on a time and place, the chair should then write a letter to each individual and group inviting them to attend the organizational meeting to form a coalition. The letter should briefly state the concerns about arts education and give the meeting date, time, place, and any special instructions. Enclose copies of the reports assessing arts education and arts resources in the community, as well as a tentative agenda. After mailing the letter, the committee chair should make brief follow-up calls to get initial reactions and to encourage attendance.

At the first coalition meeting, designate a person to lead the meeting and someone to take notes. Have representatives briefly tell the group their name, the group they represent, the philosophy of their group toward arts education, whom they serve, and what their capabilities are. Invite them to offer suggestions toward the common goal of meeting the Standards, and to discuss what projects they have that address the needs for improving arts education.

As soon as each organization has formally joined the coalition, decisions on structure and procedures can be made and tasks assigned. Elect officers, select a name for the coalition, and develop a brief mission statement (organizers may want to bring a proposed draft). Identify and list the barriers that must be overcome. Based on the list of barriers, identify specific tasks that must be accomplished for the coalition to succeed; for example, a public information campaign may be necessary. Divide into groups to accomplish specific tasks. Each group should be responsible for developing its own plan of action and a

tentative time line for executing it. Each group should report on its activities to the full coalition membership.

The following are a few additional suggestions for possible coalition strategies that could be used as part of the action plans.

◆ Adopt a slogan and use it with a media campaign. South Carolina's The Arts in the Basic Curriculum Project, for example, developed public service announcements and printed materials, including bumper stickers, around the slogan "Arts Education in South Carolina Means Business." It has been highly successful statewide.

◆ Hold press conferences when needed.

◆ Have designated spokespeople appear on talk shows at every opportunity to promote the Standards.

◆ Sponsor a rally in support of arts education and the Standards. Hold the rally on the steps of the state capitol, city hall, or the district office. Make this a positive event that focuses on the good results of quality arts education. The rally should happen at the time decisions about arts education are being made or considered. Get media coverage.

◆ Ask the governor, mayor, or chairperson of the county council or school board to proclaim "Arts Education Month."

◆ Hold a statewide or community function to celebrate the arts.

◆ Bring in celebrities to publicize support for the Standards.

◆ Send articles to magazines for publication and letters to the editors of local and state newspapers in support of the Standards.

♦ Develop curriculum frameworks for the arts based on the Standards, and ask the state department of education to adopt and implement them. (This strategy should be executed in collaboration with professionals in K–12 curriculum and higher-education representatives, not parents—unless they are specifically trained.)

♦ Advocate adoption and implementation of the frameworks.

As with any worthwhile project, using these strategies to adopt the Standards will not be an easy task. It will take hard work, dedication, and many hours of volunteer time. But once the Standards are adopted, involved parents will know that they made a positive difference in the lives of all children educated in the system. One person or group operating alone cannot be effective, but working together, parents can accomplish the goal of implementing the National Standards for Arts Education in every school in America.

Kitty Waikart, a parent from Columbia, South Carolina, is the chairman of the Cultural Arts Committee of the National PTA.

Building Support for the Arts Standards among School Administrators

Benjamin O. Canada

" **A** rt begins with resistance—at the point where resistance is overcome. No human masterpiece has ever been created without great labor." These words of André Gide, written to François Mauriac in 1928, speak directly to the implementation of the National Standards for Arts Education. There will be resistance to national standards. It will have to be confronted by superintendents and curriculum coordinators, by principals and assistant principals.

Resistance will take many forms. Administrators, not trained to view the arts as basic, will hold back because they have failed to create parental support for arts education. Many state departments of education have failed to develop curriculum frameworks for the arts, and state assessments in the arts are lacking.

In many cases, collaborative arrangements between state departments of education and teacher-training institutions, and between them and local school districts, are lacking. Preservice and in-service training for teachers of the arts does not support arts education well, especially in theatre and dance.

There will be resistance in state legislatures where, in many states, the value of arts education for all students is not supported. Even at the school board level, most boards tend to equate quality education with mere competence in reading, writing, and arithmetic, combined with improvements in performance on national tests.

Other forms of resistance will arise from the lack of community-level coordination between state and local arts agencies and school administrators. At the national level, few professional education organizations have made Standards part of their national agendas.

Finally, and perhaps most tragically, resistance will take the form of stereotyping poor and minority children, blocking their access to meaningful arts programs. How is the resistance to be overcome?

Increasing Administrators' Understanding of the Arts' Value

The first approach to overcoming administrators' lack of knowledge about the value of arts programs is to educate them. Here, the Standards speak clearly. They offer a benchmark against which administrators can project expectations of what it means to be an "educated" student; they also offer clear statements of the knowledge and skills such students must be able to demonstrate. If administrators are not given in-service education on the role the arts can play in helping students become truly educated, the arts will continue to take a back seat. State departments of education and state school board associations need to establish requirements for in-service programs in the arts for all administrators, and such programs should be administered as a part of the annual certification requirements for those administrators. In particular, administrator in-services should address both the value of arts education and practical ways of implementing the Standards.

A collaborative effort between state departments of education and school board associations would send a strong, clear signal of the priority that each places upon the arts. For most administrators, such a signal would be enough to generate the interest needed to move reform forward. But none of this can be accomplished without state departments first creating curricular frameworks that include arts as a vital part of the basic curriculum. Such a framework would be incomplete, however, without the assessment and accountability mechanisms needed to support it.

State Curriculum Frameworks for Arts Education

Every state in the nation has some system of accreditation, including frameworks for curricula, for its school districts and the schools within them. Most state accreditation standards say very little about arts curricula, however. This lack means that school boards, superintendents, and local administrators usually devote very little time and few resources to arts education. To combat this, it will be necessary for state departments of education—and perhaps state legislatures—to do the following:

♦ State emphatically that a specific requirement for competency in arts education is essential for every child. This statement should encompass each grade level and would be met through instruction in dance, music, theatre, and the visual arts.

♦ Emphasize the need to incorporate the arts in other academic subjects at the elementary and middle school levels, while pushing for major areas of concentration and competence in one of the arts at the high school level.

♦ Form an alliance with state school boards and local boards of education to develop strategies for implementing the arts Standards at local, state, and national levels.

♦ Create a climate and a plan for local boards to defend greater allocations of time and resources for the arts. This will provide an open door for collaboration with colleges and universities in helping to develop the teaching force needed to implement the Standards. School districts and state departments of education need to demand different programs for college and university teacher preparation programs dealing with the arts.

Preservice and In-Service Education in the Arts

Local school administrators would welcome new models for teacher education. While the idea of using the arts for this purpose may seem foreign, some catalyst is certainly required to change the model we now have. A host of state and local forums for teachers, administrators, college and university representatives, citizens, and legislators is needed to assess both current training programs and their results in terms of arts education. From such forums can come the energy to ignite reform of the teacher-education model now in use.

Local school districts should cease the practice of signing off on grant applications promoted by colleges and universities unless there is abiding evidence that the institution is willing and able to make meaningful changes in its teacher-preparation program. The practice of writing letters of support for grants, yet never fully discussing the grant and its impact on the local school district until it is time for reapplication, must stop.

Local PTA and other support groups need to lobby legislators to fund post-graduate teacher-training programs for classroom teachers and school administrators. Those specific lobbying efforts must insist that teaching the arts is basic to quality teacher preparation, and the credo of such an effort must be that teachers educated in the arts are necessary to educate children in the arts. Local school districts and their advocates should use the power of the media (flyers, ads in newspapers and on local radio and television, and any other available forum) to advocate preservice and in-service teacher education as essential to the success of a well-educated child. In particular, advocates must challenge the idea that the only time a teacher is "working" is when he or she is standing in front of a class. Developing professional skills occupies 10 percent of the work year of most business executives; the same should be true of teachers. Once these steps are taken, we will begin to see both arts education and the Standards on the front burner of the national education associations.

Preparation of this kind cannot be accomplished without broad-based support. In speeches to local service organizations, committed administrators must constantly remind community leaders and decision makers of the need to upgrade teachers' knowledge and skills.

Professional Education Organizations

The National Standards for Arts Education have not yet had time to become part of the national agenda for many professional organizations. But that time has arrived. Until now, state and local affiliates of those national organizations have not viewed arts education as being important enough to warrant such attention. But that can change, if local educator-members do a better job of translating their concerns about implementing the Standards into agenda items at local chapter meetings, state meetings, and national conventions and conferences.

Articles in professional journals, especially regarding research that demonstrates the value of arts education in preparing young people with the cognitive skills necessary for today's workplace, will help create a climate of support for arts education from local business owners; such support is clearly in their interest.

Legislative Support

Legislative mandates without the resources to fulfill them are a way of life for most school administrators. The lot of the arts, however, has not been lack of funding; they have simply been ignored by legislators and administrators alike. The best way to combat this mindset is through the kind of collaborative arrangements discussed above, involving state departments of education, state school board associations, colleges and universities, PTA and other parent organizations, business leaders, retirees, and other organized groups. These groups can make an impact on legislative bodies.

Part of the argument of these groups must be grounded in the more obvious and dramatic concerns of legislators.

Many districts have found, for example, that children who are engaged in arts activities develop better study habits, are able to set goals, and are better managers of their own time in meeting those goals. This information—and the research to back it up—belongs on the desks of state legislators as they vote more funds to put metal detectors and antiviolence programs into schools. This is not to say that the answer to violence in the schools is arts programs; it is to say that children have been shown to respond positively when expectations—such as those provided by the Standards—are raised. It is also to say that the child who cannot be reached in history class may well be reached in the art studio or the rehearsal hall. Well-rounded arts programming can only increase the likelihood of success with these problems. But collaborative efforts to create such programming must come from the schools, with the leadership of committed administrators.

Parental Involvement

The importance of parental involvement in any aspect of education cannot be overstated, and with respect to implementing the Standards, parents are perhaps the most important factor in the whole equation. If parents do not view the school as seeking and using their ideas and energy, they will not support the efforts of the school district on any front.

Administrators whose view of parental involvement is limited to a quarterly meeting, the fall PTA reception, or the Booster Club fund drive for new band uniforms are wasting a valuable resource. Real parental involvement also means including nontraditional partners in school decision making. Who are these nontraditional partners? Some are parents of poor and minority children, who have been excluded from active involvement in the schools by oversight or by design. Parent volunteers, community mentors, and members of partners-in-education programs are also nontraditional partners who belong in the local school's decision-making process.

One mechanism for recruiting nontraditional partners is an annual, school-sponsored forum to set goals for the graduates of the school district who happen to be born in the current year. Such a forum requires that the local school district and its community think well beyond the narrow confines of its existing pupil base and in longer-range terms than the next few years. In looking toward the future, the community begins a learning process that helps it analyze what it wants, how it proposes to achieve it, and what it will take to achieve it.

Using the Standards as a part of the community review of curriculum requirements for future graduates helps direct the community's attention beyond the school as the single source for securing a quality education. It teaches the lesson that creating an educated student is the responsibility of the entire community. The results of such community planning forums must be disseminated in a way that generates standards and expectations, both within the school district and

in the broader community. Backed by such community involvement, local school boards and administrators can take a broader view of what "quality education" means, and the arts can then become a part of "a basic education."

Local School Boards

Arts education has not been at the top of many school board agendas over the years. This can be explained in part by the education those board members themselves received. If their own education backgrounds included the arts, they are much more likely to view the arts as a viable and valuable part of the general curriculum; similarly, such members are far more likely to support implementation of the arts Standards. To enlist the support of board members who do not currently value arts education, it will be necessary to educate them.

The education of school board members can begin with their active participation in state and national school board organizations. Members who venture beyond the scope of the local board meeting acquire a much broader view of what constitutes a quality education. State-level training of local school board members is also essential to an understanding of what constitutes sound education policy; this should be a statutory priority in all states. Armed with sound information and substantive parental involvement, it is far more likely that local school boards will establish policies to ensure that local administrators give the arts the attention they deserve.

The Standards must become a priority of the school board, but a bigger issue must be faced by school boards before that can happen. The value of even the best of arts education programs at the local level is tarnished when access to them is restricted by stereotypes. Nowhere is this more evident than in the stereotypes that control the educational destiny of poor and minority children.

Stereotypes of Poor and Minority Children

During every school day, school teachers and school administrators in more than fifteen thousand school districts throughout America ought to challenge the idea that poor children, regardless of race or ethnicity, need only "basic skills programs."

◆

The value of even the best of arts education programs at the local level is tarnished when access to them is restricted by stereotypes.

◆

Children of the poor are, first of all, children; they have the same capacity as other children for appreciating and benefiting from the arts. They, too, can have their intellectual skills stretched and their skills improved; they, too, can become actively engaged; they, too, can become problem solvers and creative thinkers. Administrators who do not believe this should ask themselves why.

The view that these children do not know how to appreciate the arts, and that the only way such an appreciation can be built is on the foundation of "the basics," leads to a propensity for drill and practice; it also leaves little or no time for engagement in arts programs. Though drill and practice quickly become "drill and kill," field trips and curricula that offer exposure and hands-on experiences in dance, music, theatre, and the visual arts are too often beyond the imagination of many educators in areas where there is a high concentration of poor and minority children.

School administrators can do much to combat this stereotyping. School districts need to inform teachers of the kinds of arts programs that are available through field experiences. District funds for field trips must then be allocated with the clear expectation that some of them must be used for arts experiences in the community.

It should be noted, however, that field trips cannot be used as the sole means of meeting the Standards. Field trips are a valid part of a comprehensive arts curriculum, not a substitute for it. For their part, teachers and administrators should receive meaningful opportunities to participate in nationally recognized in-service and professional-development programs in the arts that involve representatives from poor and minority communities.

Schools should be encouraged to create opportunities for student exhibitions and performances for community organizations, religious groups, business groups, service clubs, and any other forums that expose the community to the outstanding educational results of study in the arts disciplines. The community should be invited to visit classrooms to witness the high caliber of the school arts curriculum in action.

Creating the Masterpiece

Implementing the arts Standards is but one aspect of providing a quality education for all children; nevertheless, it will be a fundamental, enduring, and essential aspect of that process. The suggestions made in this article will naturally require additional funding. The temptation will be to say that because all the standards in all the academic areas cannot be implemented at once, no action should be taken. But that would be wrong. In most communities, funds will continue to be limited for the foreseeable future. Development of a plan that includes a time line for full implementation is thus essential to any form of community support. One cannot complete a journey without starting out.

Full implementation of the Standards will require nothing less than a political and administrative masterpiece, one requiring far greater imagination than we have shown in the past. It will require an outpouring of labor and involvement by a much greater population of nontraditional participants in the decision processes that affect a child's education. But school administrators have a history of creating masterpieces, of finding the precise point where resistance ends and creativity begins. I believe that this creativity can be brought to bear on implementing the Standards. Our labor as administrators will, as always, overcome the resistance, so we can look ahead with some confidence to the time when the masterpiece has been completed. But we must believe that we can complete the task, and we must be willing to put our energies to work where our imagination leads. Our students deserve nothing less. The words of Gide are as appropriate here as they were at the beginning: "Art begins with resistance—at the point where resistance is overcome. No human masterpiece has ever been created without great labor."

Benjamin O. Canada is superintendent of schools of the Jackson Public School District in Jackson, Mississippi.

Involving School Boards in Implementing the Arts Standards

Nancy Jo Johnson

Implementing the National Standards for Arts Education will take time and the collaboration of many constituencies, both in the arts community and in the schools. Among them, none will play a more crucial role than the local school board. Indeed, it is no overstatement to assert that any attempts to improve arts education that do not involve local school boards and community members will surely fail.

Before the goal of implementing the Standards can be accomplished, it must have broad-based local support. This article identifies six barriers that can get in the way of successful implementation of the arts Standards.

This article also offers two kinds of suggestions: how to reach school board members and how to encourage them to become actively involved in overcoming these barriers.

The barriers include the community's perception of the arts, funding, accountability, qualified educators, equity, and time.

The Community's Perception of the Arts

Many community members continue to view the arts and arts education as something for the elitist, a frill, the narrow interest of a special interest group, or a curricular area relevant only to gifted and talented children. Even amid current pressures on local school boards to "get back to the basics," the definitions of those basics rarely include the arts. Many still view the arts as black-tie evenings at the theatre or symphony—not as CDs, movies, or the artistic effort that shapes literally every manufactured object in our environment. To gain broad support for including arts curricula as a "basic" in public schools, opportunities must be identified that will consistently increase understanding of the value of the arts to students and communities.

Arts advocates need to create a more comprehensive and compelling presentation of the arts, one that informs the public that the arts are far more than a finished product that entertains or pleases the senses. They must define and describe the arts as a basic part of life and thus of the school curriculum. Professionals in the arts must develop exciting movements in classrooms and schools that create surges of positive interest that can spread throughout the community.

Funding

Funding in general, and of arts programs in particular, continues to be a barrier for many school districts. Resources are finite. In some communities the support for public education is lessening, as citizens feel they are being taxed excessively. Unfunded state and federal mandates take dollars away from educational programs and put them into noneducational areas. In many areas, school safety has become an overwhelming concern. Even where there is a positive predisposition toward the goals of the arts Standards, sympathy for implementation will wane if it is unaccompanied by resources. Absent those resources, strong resistance to implementation from school officials is predictable.

One way of working on this problem is for school boards to encourage school-based partnerships with state and local arts councils. Many states have found that council-supported artist-in-residence programs get more artists into classrooms, who in turn stimulate greater enthusiasm for arts programs. Local or state arts councils can also develop a lending library of instructional videos and materials. Partnerships with

the business community are a further possibility; these relationships could go beyond requests for monetary gifts and services to open discussions and linkages that benefit both parties. In North Dakota, for example, the Fargo School District developed a corporate art-lease program. Students' visual art works are appropriately framed, displayed, and periodically rotated among participating businesses. Leasing fees from this program go toward continuing the program and toward the general arts program to purchase materials and other resources that support instruction.

School board policy on arts instruction must be sufficiently flexible so that, whenever possible, teachers can create opportunities to showcase students' learning by having art shows, theatre performances, and concerts for parents and the public. A caution is in order, however. In the study of the arts, process and product go together. Students learn concepts, intellectual skills, and the techniques of the arts disciplines; they do not just put on a performance or create a final project. If arts programs are not handled carefully—that is, if only final products are seen—the community may well decide it can do without them. The valuable learning process that creates the product is then lost as well.

Accountability

Another area of concern for school board members is accountability. How do we determine what arts education accomplishes for students in schools?

How do we relate education in the arts to overall excellence in education? Standardized test results are frequently used as a measure or indication of excellence, but these are of only limited value in assessing the results of arts education. How, after all, does a multiple-choice test measure the ability to meet artistic criteria demonstrated in painting a watercolor, playing the clarinet, or acting in *Our Town?* Arts advocates need to work more assertively with local school boards to establish minimal arts requirements, as well as the best assessment tools, to measure growth and learning in the products *and* processes of the arts. Otherwise, only the students who are best at "producing" will be recognized; the rest will be ignored.

Many school boards and state legislatures are looking at ways to measure learner outcomes at the local level. Assessments for the arts may well meld better with assessment programs for other subjects.

Qualified Educators

If every school district were to adopt the Standards right away, the first result would be an across-the-board shortage of qualified educators in the arts disciplines. Many elementary classroom teachers would not be fully competent to provide the instruction their students need to meet the Standards. It will be expensive for a local school system to devise and conduct in-service programs for all its staff. Even if the community desires a comprehensive arts program, readjusting funding priorities will create

its own problems.

Finding qualified arts educators begins with teacher preparation programs in higher education. The present system does not encourage or require individuals preparing to teach in elementary schools, for example, to develop the knowledge or skills needed to fully incorporate the arts into their classroom. Arts advocates and local school boards must work together in urging teacher preparation institutions to include appropriate arts requirements as basic components for teacher preparation and to base those requirements on the Standards. In the effort to bring potential teachers into higher education better prepared to become knowledgeable about the arts, colleges and universities should also require arts credits for high school graduates as a condition for admission.

Teacher organizations also need to place a higher value on the place of arts education in the curriculum. To gain the support of classroom teachers, people working toward implementing the arts Standards must be responsive to teachers' concerns and help find ways to address them as part of the implementation process. If advocates can show how arts education helps achieve established educational objectives and addresses broader school concerns, arts programs will gain greater acceptance by local school boards and the general public.

Administrators, too, need to develop a greater awareness of the value of arts programming. State departments of education can play a vital leadership role in this area. They can provide financial support for staff development programs for administrators that address the value of the arts, demonstrate the academic rigor of arts study, and show how the arts can enhance learning across the curriculum. Administrators' recommendations go a long way toward encouraging school boards to initiate or continue support of arts programs.

Equity

Equity will be a big concern for school boards as they seek to implement the Standards. Often inner-city, minority, or rural students lack consistent opportunities for firsthand experiences in the arts. Greater use of local artists through artist-in-residence programs can prove helpful: these programs certainly help students, and teachers can benefit as well when the programs include in-service education.

Some school districts have already begun using distance learning and interactive television to bring arts classrooms to students. This approach also offers much promise for in-service for teachers and should be encouraged.

Time

Demands on time within the school day, with all the requirements already laid on teachers and administrators, constitute a real hindrance to implementation. Time-saving approaches—for example, providing materials for pre- and post-visit classes as part of artist-in-residence programs—are valuable to teachers. Some educational publishers provide suggestions for related experi-

ences in the arts in their teacher guides and texts; skilled teachers can incorporate these suggestions into the unit. Publishers should be encouraged to continue this emphasis on the arts.

The time problem can also be attacked if school districts are granted the option of using the new Standards for ideas and direction when developing an arts curriculum, in collaboration with state-developed curriculum guides. Again, if the community's perception is strong, positive, and supportive, the local school board will be more receptive to an effort to achieve greater balance in the eternal tug-of-war between time and revenue.

Working with the Board

Lay school board members are elected both to represent and to shape the views of the community. They may not necessarily be knowledgeable about the arts or what the benefits of arts programs can be. School board membership also changes regularly. Most terms are three to four years, but many board members stay for only one term because of the complexity of the issues they have to contend with. Professionals in arts education, therefore, have a strong role to play in both educating board members and recommending appropriate policy options for boards to consider.

How can maximum support be garnered from school board members? This, too, is a process of continual education. A national discussion of the arts Standards, arts education, and the development of a better-balanced curriculum should be launched among school board members at local, state, and national levels. A demonstration classroom at a state or national convention attended by school board members, for example, would provide board members with firsthand contact and experience. It would be an opportunity for local school board members to see students engaged in the arts, instead of just hearing about how students learn the arts. Arts education advocacy groups should also establish speakers' bureaus and send representatives to talk to communities and school boards on the value of arts education. Most school board meetings have community comment periods; arts advocates can use these to make the board aware of their issues and concerns. Students can perform at board meetings or special gatherings, and mount displays of their art work in board rooms and in community buildings. Concerts and public presentations can be used to endorse the arts while community, parents, and school staff are in attendance. The more visibility arts education receives, the more people will understand its value.

School board members have a responsibility of their own to become familiar with research results on the benefits of the arts as a basic part of the curriculum; arts advocates can help them in this task. One-on-one visits with school board members, away from "official" contexts, to talk about what the arts Standards mean, how they could be used, and how they could benefit students could be very helpful. Students can talk to board members, too; it is more difficult for a board member to decline an invitation to an arts event from a student than to "take a pass" on an open invitation. Board members should also be encouraged to visit classrooms, not just to observe performances and the results of projects, but to observe the processes of arts education. Better yet, let board members get involved themselves.

Full implementation of the Standards will not take place quickly, but there will be a lot of opportunity for advocates to see success. For its part, the National School Boards Association, whose Delegate Assembly went on record in 1993 in support of voluntary arts Standards, plans to continue to work to implement the Standards and arts curricula in the schools, through its clinics, presentations, and annual conferences. As perceptions gradually change, communities will start to support the arts with funding, time, and personnel. Because the desire for implementation will not come from mandates, local board initiatives are important: The funding and community commitment needed to create the foundation for local implementation begins with them. Once school board members embrace the value of the arts, that value will take on its own life, to the benefit of all students.

Nancy Jo Johnson is a member of the Board of Education in Dickinson, North Dakota; president of the North Dakota School Boards Association; and serves on the Board of Directors of the National School Boards Association.

Implementing the Standards
Making Use of the Arts Community

Robert L. Lynch

The arts community can and must play a key partnership role in the work to ensure that comprehensive, balanced, sequential programs of arts education, taught by qualified teachers, exist in the schools of every American community. The arts community must also be a key partner in ensuring that these programs incorporate the National Standards for Arts Education.

Correspondingly, those who advocate implementing the Standards and who have an education background need to understand the most effective ways of partnering with the arts community. The goal of that partnership is more easily stated than achieved, for it will mean facing and overcoming a number of issues and obstacles. They include, among others:

♦ the identity issues and agenda of the arts community itself
♦ the curious lack of real support for the arts in American society, which declares itself so forthrightly in favor of the arts and arts education
♦ the perception that financial support for arts education may erode support for the arts themselves
♦ the competing voices and visions in the arts and arts education, and the need for central sources for resources, information, success stories, and models
♦ the perception among many arts groups that in advocacy efforts for the arts, and even arts education, the arts education people don't come through.

Each of these obstacles is discussed below, and some specific overall long-term strategies are provided for addressing them, with a view toward the goal of making the arts a basic part of education in all schools, based on implementation of the Standards.

Identity and Agenda Issues

To begin, the term "arts community" is misleading. It certainly does not exist as an identifiable, single entity in American cultural life. Nor does the term designate a group of people who share an outlook, goals, or perspectives. The arts community is perhaps best understood loosely as the entire spectrum of individuals and organizations that create art and support the arts. It includes large, nonprofit institutions such as museums, theaters, opera companies, dance companies, symphonies, major art centers, and presenter organizations. It also encompasses small, struggling arts organizations in every discipline, ethnically based arts groups, experimental galleries and performance places, folk festivals, and every imaginable combination of all these. The arts community also includes organizations that focus on the arts needs of the consuming public and arts producers. In this sense, the arts community includes state arts councils, local arts agencies, regional arts organizations, the National Endowment for the Arts, and others. Finally, the term embraces individual artists and parts of the for-profit arts world. These groups constitute more of an "arts list" than an "arts community."

Among the difficulties of so disparate a group are differing needs and competing agendas, which vary radically among its members. But what these people and groups generally share is a belief that the arts are vitally important to America and the conviction, often grounded in experience, that the arts are not properly appreciated or well supported.

Concern for Self-Survival. Each art form or branch of the arts community has its own problems; naturally enough, solving those problems is of primary importance to those who have them. The arts community suffers from an interesting mix of deprivation and success. The successful part is that in just the last twenty-eight years, the arts, not including arts education, have experienced tremendous growth. For example, in that time period, there was a 1,215 percent increase in the number of professional dance companies and a 650 percent increase in the number of nonprofit theatre companies. During the same period, public support for the arts from the combined federal, state, and local government levels grew from almost nothing to around $2 billion. Today, the nonprofit arts industry alone contributes some $36.8 billion in direct expenditures to the nation's economy and supports 1.3 million jobs. On the other hand, economic problems have seriously hurt the arts in recent years. Twenty-five professional theatres have closed their doors since 1988. Both state and federal funding for the arts have been cut back, while private-sector support for the arts has been at a virtual standstill. In this atmosphere, the tendency toward an attitude of self-survival is strong; the needs and well-being of other arts groups slide down the list of things to be concerned about.

The Needs and Agenda of the Arts Community

The arts community has come to believe that, despite this growth, there is a grave lack of understanding and appreciation for the arts in every possible sector and at every level of American society. Although that is a strong statement, it is nonetheless true. Despite the existence of some key public and private-sector supporters, who have never flagged, support remains precarious and uneven, whether from individual patron donors, tickets at the box office, business leaders who oversee corporate coffers, or government officials who guard the public purse.

In the face of this uncertainty, the arts community has seen an immediate need for massive efforts to secure better visibility about the value and relevance of the arts and stronger lobbying for support for the arts. This need has resulted, for example, in the creation of the National Cultural Alliance, a five-year, $25 million visibility effort involving the National Ad Council and more than fifty national arts- and humanities-service organizations, representing more than twenty-six thousand local arts and humanities organizations. There is also a wider recognition that the lack of basic arts education in our nation's schools lies at the core of the problems of under-appreciative audiences, the lack of donors, and the indifference of some elected leaders to the arts. In this regard, the inclusion of the arts in the Goals 2000: Educate America Act and the publication of *National Standards for Arts Education* are the first, hopeful steps of a journey in a new direction.

This is not to say, however, that no work is needed to convince the arts community of the value of arts education and the Standards. Indeed, part of any campaign to adopt and implement the Standards must begin by working toward a dramatic change in attitude among artists, arts administrators, arts patrons, and board members of local arts organizations about the role and value of arts education.

Clarifying What We Mean by Arts Education

Although *support* for the arts is often uncertain, there are clear indicators in polls and surveys that Americans value the arts and want an arts education for their children. In a 1991 Harris poll, for example, nearly seven out of ten respondents said they would be willing to see cuts in administrative spending in their local schools to provide more support for arts education; astonishingly, more than half said they would support cutting back school athletics programs to do so.

But aside from some isolated efforts, there has, until now, been no simple message or goal to rally behind. It has not been clear to the public just what constitutes arts education. The term has been used for efforts that range from strong proposals for extensive education in a single art form, to efforts that only promote artists-in-the-schools programs, to efforts that combine certified teachers with community resources. One of the significant advantages of the Standards document is that it provides clear statements about what constitutes an arts education through the K–12 spectrum. It covers the four arts disciplines of dance, music, theatre, and the visual arts, and it offers highly specific statements about both content and achievement. Taken together, the Standards provide a welcome statement of what an arts education means, not just in theory but in terms of what should happen in classrooms.

Given this mandate, the arts community, disparate as it is, can and will add implementation of these Standards to its advocacy agenda. The consortium of arts organizations that produced the Standards (the American Alliance for Theatre & Education, the Music Educators National Conference, the National Art Education Association, and the National Dance Association) should be joined in advocacy by other arts education organizations, other arts education leaders such as The John F. Kennedy Center for the Performing Arts, the J. Paul Getty Trust, the National Endowment for the Arts, and, indeed, by the whole arts community, perhaps represented by the National Cultural Alliance.

Competing Voices and Visions

One of the most serious obstacles for the whole arts community derives, paradoxically, from one of its greatest strengths—its great diversity. It is difficult for the arts community as a whole, or any particular arts group whose support for the Standards is being enlisted, to distinguish between competing visions of what arts education is or what priorities are most important. Basic agreement on the Standards by all major groups in the arts and arts education communities will go a long way toward solving this problem. The Standards can thus become the banner to which arts organi-

zations and artists can rally, a clear set of principles that can be presented in resolution form to, and adopted by, all national arts organizations. If a central body such as the National Coalition for Education in the Arts (NCEA), already a forum for a national dialogue about arts education, could help solidify such a consensus, that would be a true service. Indeed, the NCEA has already moved down that road by producing such useful working papers as "A Definition of Arts Education" and "Advocacy through Partnership: Advancing the Case for Arts Education."

A further difficulty lies in how the arts are used in arts education. There continues to be a perception (or misperception) that the arts education community does not necessarily value the contributions of artists and arts organizations in arts education, and that some arts education leaders are reluctant to make use of working artists as an adjunct to a sequential instructional program. The arts community outside the schools will rally in support of the Standards more readily as it becomes clearer to them that the Standards allow for true collaboration, combining the resources of a working partnership of certified teachers, professional artists, community-based arts organizations, and others who can make a significant contribution.

Information Source. Also lacking at the moment is a single source of information for success stories and educational models in the arts. The Arts Education Partnership Working Group, convened and sponsored by The John F. Kennedy

Center for the Performing Arts; the J. Paul Getty Trust; and ArtsEdge, the National Arts and Education Information Network housed at the Kennedy Center, already act in this capacity, but not in a coordinated way. With such a mechanism, all national arts service organizations and local arts organizations, as well as arts educators, could access the same information about successful models, successful efforts at Standards implementation, changing ideas, and new curricula, pedagogy, and resources. A clearinghouse for information would contribute significantly to a sense of unity in arts education nationwide.

One of the difficulties that a unified Standards implementation effort will have to counter squarely is the perception that financial support for arts education threatens support for the arts themselves. Community arts organizations have seen their funding sources increasingly under attack, primarily from two directions. First, the recent controversies over art pieces characterized by some as pornographic or blasphemous have taken their toll on arts funding and on the goodwill of some segments of the public. Second, the recent uncertain state of the economy has unleashed increasingly effective arguments that the arts are somehow an unessential expense—an argument often used by extension against arts education as well. The one bright light has been that in arts-funding discussions, elected officials have spoken more highly about arts education than ever before. A united, collaborative effort behind arts education that

incorporates the academically strong arts education represented in the Standards, along with the enhancement opportunities provided by the broader arts community, would go a long way toward countering these two negatives.

Another hindrance to an all-out effort to support the Standards is the perception that, when the chips are down, arts education people don't come through. Whether true or not, the perception of many arts organizations is that when it comes time for lobbying local school boards and state legislatures, the arts groups are there but arts educators are not, even to support their own programs. The related perception is that there is no quid pro quo—that when efforts are needed for support for the arts themselves, the arts educators are not part of that effort. Surely, however, the reverse is also true. Arts educators often feel abandoned when their education programs are under attack, and that they receive only token support from the arts community.

There is only one solution to this problem. Arts educators and local arts organizations have to work together to prove their perceptions of one another not so much untrue as irrelevant. The standards movement in American education reform is a tremendous opportunity for arts education. It cannot be seized unless people on all sides roll up their sleeves and pitch in. Better communication among groups may help clear up misconceptions, but a united partnership for advocacy and visibility is absolutely essential.

Strategies

Success in implementing the Standards will depend on many factors. What is necessary, first, is a massive, multitiered effort aimed at decision makers who themselves are undereducated about the value of the arts, arts education, and the Standards. The effort will have to be both vertical and horizontal—that is, it will have to be vertically multitiered, existing simultaneously at national, state, and local levels of the decision-making hierarchy; as well as horizontal, targeting the spectrum of decision makers and constituency groups at national, state, and local levels who have a stake in arts education and the place of the arts in our society.

This multitiered strategy especially includes targeting decision makers and potential advocates at each level of their professional involvement, in their state and national professional associations. At the local level, this spectrum of decision makers includes elected officials such as mayors, city council members, county commissioners; members of the education community such as superintendents, school boards, PTAs, and teachers; and other key decision makers such as city managers, business leaders, and the arts community, including arts councils, institutions, and individual artists. National success in implementing the Standards will be achieved only if all of these local decision-making groups are targeted and involved.

What the Arts Community Can Do. "All politics is local," as Tip O'Neill said. In a given locale, the members of the arts community, if rallied as a unified group, can be quite effective. For example, in a hypothetical, mid-sized community, there might be a symphony, perhaps an opera company, several theatres, a museum, a dance company, a variety of smaller music organizations, folk art groups, several ethnically centered arts groups, a variety of individual artists and performers, some neighborhood arts centers, several commercial arts enterprises (music stores, art galleries), and a community arts council (the city's local arts agency). Together, this group can be a powerful force pushing for the implementation of the Standards.

Networks, Networks, Networks. Ideally, the arts council would try to provide service to all these groups, but the lead could also be taken by any of the arts organizations in the mix. In some cases, a particular arts organization may have the history and credibility to emerge as the natural leader. But for any group to take action, they need to know about the Standards in the first place. Here is where the vertical dimension comes into play. In the case of the local arts agency, which is my own particular field of expertise and involvement, there are thirty-five statewide organizations of local arts agencies; there is also a national association, the National Assembly of Local Arts Agencies (NALAA). If NALAA were convinced to pass a resolution adopting the Standards officially, and if it were persuaded to train its members in how to implement them, and if statewide organizations and arts agencies did the same, then the network, the "buy-in," and the information flow would be taken care of at every level.

Considering that almost every other group mentioned in the mix of local groups also has a national if not a statewide organization (for example, the American Symphony Orchestra League, Opera America, Dance/USA, Artists Equity, the National Association of Artist Organizations), this is a far-flung network. The state arts agency network—with its national organization, the National Assembly of State Arts Agencies—is also in touch on a state-by-state basis with all its local organizations. The typical arts agency will have a designated staff for the state arts education effort and for community development; these staff members will themselves be part of their own national networks. Finally, add in the national organizations with programs specifically geared to schools, such Young Audiences, the Kennedy Center, and the National Endowment for the Arts. These organizations also have local networks. The list could go on and on.

Success in facilitating action in this arts-community network depends heavily, however, on the following:

♦ Everyone must be clear about what is being asked of him or her so that action, not talk, is the result.

♦ Tasks must be simple and achievable.

♦ Information must reach the people who can take the action.

♦ "Buy-in" must be achieved by get-

ting groups to specifically commit both to the Standards and to an implementation plan, perhaps through a resolution adoption process at the national, state, and local levels.

♦ A generic action kit of materials and step-by-step action procedures should be created so that maximum time can be spent on taking action rather than on reinventing strategies. Materials should be prepared to respond to predictable arguments such as "Why should we even try when we know these Standards cannot be achieved?"

♦ Communication must be continuing and regular. As a starting point, both the National Coalition for Education in the Arts and the National Cultural Alliance should take a role in fostering information flow, beginning with meetings of their member arts groups to discuss Standards implementation.

♦ There must be a commitment to reciprocity from the arts education community at the national, state, and local levels to help the arts community secure the support commitments that it needs.

The implementation of the Standards is a key building block for creating not only quality arts education for all communities, but a richer, more vibrant arts community and a more arts-supportive and arts-knowledgeable public.

Robert L. Lynch is president and CEO of the National Assembly of Local Arts Agencies.

The Arts Education Standards

A Payoff for Business

Richard S. Gurin

♦ A high school sophomore and aspiring saxophonist signs up for Band I, only to discover that the program has been canceled for lack of funding.

♦ Japan endows a chair at Harvard in the name of John Bardeen, the American inventor who came up with the transistor in 1947.

♦ After searching for and finding one of the few new bicycles with an American brand name, a shopper finds out from a cycling magazine that the parts and frame were designed in France and Taiwan.

♦ A midwestern city lays off its only remaining full-time school art teacher.

Isolated incidents? Not by a long shot. Each points to a single, irrefutable fact: arts education in America is in trouble. Since the budget-cutting frenzy of the 1980s, the very part of the curriculum that focuses most directly on creativity and thinking skills—the well-spring of innovations in the business world—is in the most difficulty in the schools, which are graduating tomorrow's employees and entrepreneurs.

I've talked about these connections with business colleagues, who agree in principle. But when it comes down to writing checks to support the arts, or getting behind arts education programs in the local schools, they gripe about the bottom line and the need for belt tightening. The connection that matters, the one between the knowledge and skills the arts provide and the future of their own businesses, is the one connection that remains obscure.

Part of the problem is that too many people in business operate on a false set of assumptions about the arts and, consequently, about arts education. Here are some of them: The arts are educational window dressing, an extra, a luxury; the arts are an elitist enterprise best left to the "truly talented"; we should save scarce taxpayer dollars for funding education in the basics, not the arts.

This article directly challenges these assumptions and makes a counter-argument: The arts *are* basic to what it means to be an educated person, and support for the arts and arts education are in the self-interest of business. By way of preparing the argument, we take a detour to the Indonesian island of Bali, which has powerful lessons to teach about the importance of the arts and arts education to a society's well-being. After making the case for the strong relationship between business and the arts, there is a discussion of the National Standards for Arts Education and of why it is in the best interest of businesses to support them.

Declaring My Bias

First, let me put my own cards on the table. I'm a businessman. My company, Binney & Smith, makes and sells Crayola crayons, paints, and markers. Admittedly, more cuts in school arts programs would be bad for my company and employees. But the same would be true if my company made computer chips, furniture, or cat food. Because the truth is, there is not a business in America that is not in some way dependent on the arts, whether for its advertising layouts and commercials, the design of its products, or the architecture of the buildings it occupies.

After a long business career, I have become increasingly concerned that the basic problem gripping the American workplace is not interest rates or inflation; those things come and go with the business cycle. More deeply rooted is what I call the "crisis of creativity." Ideas—not sticks of colored wax, or stock

issues, or sales campaigns—are what built American businesses. And it is the arts that build ideas and nurture a place in the mind for them to grow. When a young person paints a watercolor or composes a song, his or her mind is engaged in one of the most important, intense forms of concentration known to humanity—the struggle to make something new. The abilities fostered by the arts and arts education—whether to see with a critical eye or to bring old ideas into a new relationship—overlap with the skills needed to develop new technologies and negotiate business agreements.

I know from experience that I would not have been able to make these connections for myself had it not been for my family. My mother painted; my father was a biochemist and a Juilliard-trained pianist. Along the way, my own exposure to the arts has taught me much about how others think and define their world, and I somehow picked up the strands of discipline and cooperation as well. Over the past few years, I've been coming to grips—in an everyday, business sense— with what artists have always told us, that the arts are a powerful way of knowing the world and our place in it. Paradoxically, one of the ways we can learn these lessons most forcefully is through another set of eyes—namely, the folk traditions of a more distant culture.

Detour to Bali

To prove the point, let us join a Balinese performance of *wayang* (shadow puppet theatre). It is midnight in the village, and the all-night performance is about to begin. From behind a screen, hidden puppeteers cast the shadows of intricately designed wooden puppets onto the screen, acting out an ancient and epic drama. The percussion orchestra strikes its first chord, touching off the antics of the Barong, a strange, horse-like beast (a symbol of redemption) who struggles against the evil witch Rangda and her minions. The audience cheers the performance raucously.

What may seem surprising to a Western visitor is that everyone in that audience has helped to create the performance. Some made or tuned the instruments or paid for their repairs. Others brought food. Almost everyone has attended a rehearsal. There is no sense of separation between audience and performers, as there is in our country; the idea of a "concert" as we know it is unheard of. Indeed, musicologist Christopher Small tells us that the Balinese have no word distinct for "art," or "artist," because art is not thought of as a separate activity. Art is simply a way that the Balinese concern for "doing things as well as possible" gets worked out in daily life.

The most important musical body in the *wayang* performance is the percussion orchestra, the *gamelan*. This thirty-person force interweaves melody and rhythm to produce some of the most vigorous, complex, and delicate music of all the world's traditions. There are few music "professionals" in the *gamelan*. The music is created by farmers, children, sailors, and yes, businessmen. They form clubs and play for donated funds that cover their expenses.

Gamelan rehearsals are public to enable other villagers to take part with their comments. The piece grows under the eyes of all, and the eventual performance has the same casual atmosphere as the rehearsal. It may take as long as six months to prepare. Young musicians do not learn their music in school, as our children do, or even from private teachers, but in the *gamelan*. Children begin learning as infants; parents put the mallets in their hands and guide them to the proper keys.

Today, even though tape recordings are replacing live musicians at many ceremonies, *gamelan* music remains a shared experience in the community. New clubs form constantly and new ideas quickly become common property. When a village decides to put on a show and make the necessary costumes and masks, no one talks about the venture as a bad investment or unsound business practice; the value of art is a given in Balinese society.

But what does the *gamelan* have to do with us? Just this: The arts are something a society cannot do without, and learning them is essential to the process of becoming part of society.

Challenging the Old Assumptions

To learn that lesson anew for ourselves means, first, challenging the prevailing assumption about the place of the arts in education—that they are the dessert on a curricular menu whose meat and potatoes are the three Rs. But the truth is, the arts are part of—and help to impart—the knowledge our children need to become whole human beings and to survive and compete effectively in the world economy. Arts education programs can help repair weaknesses in American education and better prepare workers for the twenty-first century.

For example, a recent compilation of more than 150 research studies, issued by the Kentucky Arts Council, shows that the arts enhance academic performance and help build the characteristics in young people that are valued by society and business alike: creativity, cooperation, and disciplined work habits. Students at schools with curricula that include more arts courses succeed at a greater rate than students at other schools. The American Council on the Arts learned through a 1991 Harris poll that students who take arts courses drop out at significantly lower rates than those who do not. More and more research points to the conclusion that studying the arts contributes to the development of what educators call "higher-order thinking skills," such as the abilities to analyze, synthesize, and evaluate information—the very skills employers say they need most of all.

Put differently, the arts are a sound business investment. When I talk with other business executives about their financial support for community arts groups and activities, they admit that the arts are likely to get the dregs. They present the case for other priorities on strictly "business" terms. "What's the

return," they ask, "on new band uniforms? Or a dance workshop?" But when I ask these executives what qualifications they look for to fill new managerial positions, the argument starts to move in the other direction. "Suppose," I say, "that two identically trained and qualified Harvard MBAs applied for the same position in your company. One has no musical background, but the other plays piano. Who would you hire?"

◆

The arts are part of—and help to impart—the knowledge our children need to become whole human beings and to survive and compete effectively in the world economy.

◆

Interestingly, most of them say they would jump at the chance to give the job to the musician. Why? Their own answers tell the story. "The work environment is changing rapidly. I look for new hires who can adapt to different ways of thinking and imagining—who are eager to learn, expressive, and open to new ideas. The combination of discipline and imagination you get from someone with a music background is hard to beat." No wonder that Willard Butcher, former chairman of Chase Manhattan Bank, has put it this way: "The kind of individual I am interested in bringing to Chase [is] one who can bring a creative outlook to the conference table."

♦

When business people support the arts and arts education, they support one of the most life-giving forces in their communities.

♦

The less able our schools are to educate our children, the more it costs business in training and retraining. So what does education in the arts have to do with building a better work force? Here are some possibilities worth considering.

♦ In the band room, young brass players learn the teamwork and cooperation that will enable them to move directly into the work management styles of the twenty-first-century corporation.

♦ A young man creating his first papier-mâché figure takes risks with formless, soggy mush, gradually learning the fundamental lesson of all the arts—that process and product are insepara-

ble. That lesson, not incidentally, lies at the core of the "total quality" concept that drives some of America's most successful companies.

♦ A young woman who has learned a series of jazz dance routines has also learned lessons about the relationship between hard work and results that will make her a much more attractive and desirable employee, the kind that most companies actively recruit.

♦ Members of the high school drama club, while studying character motivation, acquire "hands-on" experience and skills in perception and communication that are directly transferable to work relationships in the business world. Indeed, these are just the employee skills that service-oriented businesses spend millions of training dollars every year to help their employees acquire.

Arts education inspires and cultivates imagination, vision, and good judgment. The U.S. Department of Labor report, *What Work Requires of Schools* (1991), offers additional evidence. It lists the thinking skills and personal characteristics businesses want and need in their employees to stay competitive. To review that list is, in large measure, to review a list of what an education in the arts offers a young American. In other words, an education in the arts puts value into business.

The arts also improve the business climate. When business people support the arts and arts education, they support one of the most life-giving forces in their communities. Bankrolling an art exhibit or dance concert is about more than just free advertising. It is about establishing a permanent community presence that fosters enjoyment and enrichment. Why is the business–community arts partnership so effective? Because, it turns out, community members put a high value on arts education. As a 1991 Harris poll demonstrated, nine out of ten Americans believe arts education is important for their children, and three-quarters of them believe arts courses should be a part of the regular school curriculum. When business support for arts education echoes the attitudes of most Americans toward arts education, everyone benefits.

Finally, arts education generates jobs. In South Carolina, for example, arts education created more than 3,600 jobs in 1992 and was responsible for 10 to 15 percent of the economic impact of the textile and tourism industries. Nationwide, the fine arts put some $360 billion a year into the economy.

Why and How Businesses Should Support the Standards

Among the surest ways for local business people, as well as national and multinational corporations, to secure the kind of arts programs that will make the differences described above, none is more important right now than working for implementation of the National Standards for Arts Education.

Business people should have no trouble grasping the idea and the importance of the Standards. They are benchmarks, statements of what children ought to know and be able to do in the arts. They cover both content and achievement in the four arts disciplines of dance, music, theatre, and the visual arts, grades K–12. They assure that a rigorous core of academic study lies at the heart of the arts curriculum. The Standards, and the assessments related to them, will show clearly what our students are doing right in arts education and what they are doing wrong. They are the doorway to improvement; in business terms, they are part of a strategic plan for assuring quality and excellence in our schools.

In sum, students, like workers and everybody else, cannot and do not do their best unless they have high expectations; the Standards provide those expectations.

Business people can work for implementation of the Standards in many ways:

◆ One of the most effective is to use one's personal and organizational access to decision makers—for example, school board members, school administrators, local politicians, and state legislators—to lobby for adoption of the Standards as both state and local education policy.

◆ They can contact arts teachers and arts curriculum specialists in the schools to find out how they can assist in building a community-wide information and advocacy program about the Standards, reaching out especially to parents.

◆ Business people can reach out to local institutions of higher education, lending their support to what is perhaps the most critical factor in making the Standards effective: the retooling of the teaching force in America's schools to make them both literate and skilled in the teaching techniques needed to make the Standards effective in the classroom. A local business or consortium of businesses might, for example, fund a program that allows a music teacher to learn a new song repertoire or instrument, or to explore the music of another culture.

♦ Members of the business community can act as partners to local and state arts alliances in bringing the entire arts community together, as both an information source and an advocacy force for Standards implementation.

♦ On the critical issue of materials and resources to make arts programs and curricula effective, businesses can help directly through donations and sponsorship of fund-raising events. New videos, books, and interactive software can place a world of arts at a child's fingertips.

♦ Businesses and business groups, including service clubs and chambers of commerce, can become active sponsors of particular arts programs, such as a local high school dance troupe, a jazz ensemble, or an elementary school poster contest. Or, business groups could pool their resources to fund an artist-in-residence to conduct an itinerant painting or woodwinds class.

♦ Further down the road, business leaders can serve as a goad to education leaders on the crucial matter of accountability—that is, the development and administration of the kind of assessments that tell whether, and how well, the Standards are working to improve learning.

Just as the Balinese *gamelan* needs the townspeople's comments on their rehearsals, American education needs these Standards to ensure the quality of education in the arts. All of this is a tall order. To make it happen, business leaders will need to be like the Barong, the *wayang* hero, fighting against the twin evils of apathy and mediocrity. They cannot remain shadowy figures behind the screen, merely rubber-stamping programs or signing checks. They will need to take the initiative, seeking out community leaders, educators, and parents and talking with them about local needs and getting *them* to sign on the dotted line, committing themselves to making a difference in arts education. All our children—and the economy they will inherit—will be the better for it.

Richard S. Gurin is CEO of Binney & Smith. He is an active advocate for arts education to American corporations and was a member of the National Committee for Standards in the Arts, which oversaw the development of the National Standards for Arts Education.

National Standards
Implications and Strategies for the States

Barbara Kapinus, Alan Morgan, Frank Philip, Jon Quam, and Ramsay Selden

Twelve separate projects are now generating national, content-based, academic standards. In general, these projects point in the direction of three welcome results. First, they are a response to the need of both the public and the education community for a clear vision of the goals of education. Second, they are one of the richest examples of thoughtful reflection on the educational enterprise, offered by a wide range of stakeholders, that this country has experienced for many years. Third, they provide a starting point for a coordinated, coherent effort to reform and improve education at the classroom level.

National Standards for Arts Education is the result of one of the standards-writing efforts. Strategies for implementing the arts Standards are similar to those required for the other national projects, and like the other standards, they have more than implementation as their ultimate goal. At a deeper level, all the standards-writing efforts seek to leverage deep changes in the entire educational enterprise. In this article, therefore, the strategic viewpoint taken encompasses all the standards and the state role in implementing them. Where appropriate, the arts Standards are referenced specifically.

Much of our country is expressing deep concern and dissatisfaction with the education of our children. Results from the National Assessment of Educational Progress, international studies, and state-level assessments indicate that our children are not achieving as we hoped they would. Business leaders complain that high school graduates do not come to the workplace prepared to meet its high demands. Newspaper headlines of violence and greed suggest that too many children lack not only academic proficiency but also the attitudes and dispositions necessary if our communities are to enjoy peace, prosperity, and general well-being. All these developments translate into immense pressure on states to improve education dramatically.

A Systemic and Functional Approach

The reasons for this litany of problems are many, and clearly not all the answers lie in our schools. It is just as clear, however, that our schools could do far better than they are doing at present. One reason for the lack of success from many efforts to improve the schools is the continuing lack of a shared vision. Programs are established in very specific areas with little attention to how these relate to other aspects of education. Often, educational reform efforts in one place are ignorant of what has already been learned elsewhere or of what others are trying to accomplish. Worse, reform efforts wind up conflicting with one another. A systemic, coordinated approach to education reform that entails focus, direction, and coordination is needed if our schools are to achieve what the country wants and says it needs. For states, operating systemically means that policies, programs, and agencies be aligned and coordinated, instead of operating in the relative independence that prevails at present.

National standards, including the National Standards for Arts Education, afford a signal opportunity for states to focus and carefully orchestrate their improvement efforts. Standards can provide states with a clear picture of educational goals—what students should know and be able to do. States can use national standards directly, build their own standards on the results of national standards projects, or move in entirely new directions. But however they proceed with implementing standards to meet their own students' needs, all states will need to serve four major functions: information, coordination, advocacy and leadership, and technical assistance to districts and schools. Each of these functions makes a direct impact on all aspects of education, including curriculum and instruction, assessment, teacher licensure, professional development, and legislative policy. Although this article discusses each function separately, they are highly interrelated. To address one is to touch on the others.

Information. While the national standards projects have begun to provide information on their work to a wide range of stakeholders in education, it is ultimately each state education agency (SEA) that must inform districts and schools about the subject-area standards and their instructional implications. States need to make sure that educators and the public not only discuss, but help to decide, the role standards will play in setting a new direction. This review should reflect the diverse perspectives of each of the states. Where possible, states should also provide feedback to national standards projects to make certain that the standards reflect state concerns about high quality, comprehensiveness, and usability.

The basis for a sound information strategy is in using SEA staffs creatively and extensively. They must become knowledgeable about standards in all the content areas and work actively with districts and schools to help the public understand the standards fully. The logical way to develop and disseminate information is to have SEA staff members meet, as co-reviewers, with local teachers and administrators to examine the standards in depth and at length, and to consider their classroom implications. This makes the review process a part of professional development and better teacher understanding.

Coordination. States will need to coordinate their own educational improvement efforts, both within their own boundaries and with respect to national reform efforts. Here, the various standards projects offer models of how to develop standards, as well as specific content standards the states can consider in developing their own improvement efforts. In particular, states will need to coordinate the use of the various sets of standards so that interdisciplinary connections, points of unique divergence, and overall workability are considered. Some states have already articulated curriculum frameworks or a "common core of learning" to identify broader goals and encompass specific content standards. In coordinating the use of the standards, then, states will have to work toward a balance and blend of two areas: what they have already accomplished and what the standards projects are providing in the different content domains.

In planning programs and framing policies, SEAs will need to ensure communication and coordination among the players. A new assessment program, for example, should be coordinated with curriculum revisions and teacher devel-

opment programs. Here again, the standards efforts can provide a focus. Policies for teacher licensure should also reflect the impact of standards on instruction, curriculum, and assessment in institutions preparing teachers. Current projects at the Council of Chief State School Officers, such as the State Collaboratives in Assessment and Student Standards (SCASS) and the Interstate New Teacher Assessment and Support Consortium (INTASC), indicate the willingness of states to commit time and resources to this effort.

◆

States will need to coordinate their own educational improvement efforts, both within their own boundaries and with respect to national reform efforts.

◆

In some cases, states may need to reorganize their own agencies to do a better job of coordination. The comprehensiveness and challenge of the standards will require knowledgeable SEA staff to help districts and schools put the national standards to work or to implement comparable state standards. States may need to assign new staff teams specifically to these efforts or to interdisciplinary programs. In the arts, for example, SEA staff working with a local district should be familiar with curricula from related areas of literature, writing, history, and geography. State staff will also need the skills to provide technical assistance in the local setting—skills very different from the more traditional roles of monitoring and regulating. States will also need to coordinate their efforts for systemic change in designing curriculum resources and accountability mechanisms that capture the complexity of implementation.

Finally, states will need to coordinate with other groups, such as state professional organizations in the disciplines, in reviewing, analyzing, adopting, adapting, and implementing standards. Sharing this responsibility with other stakeholders is essential in generating grassroots ownership of state efforts and supplementing limited staff resources. SEAs should call on state professional groups whose national bodies have been active in developing subject-area standards to help bring together standards, implementation strategies, and the states' educational visions.

Advocacy and Leadership. States will need to model for districts and schools how standards can promote careful consideration of local goals and how they can engage a wide range of stakeholders in discussing, planning, and implementing standards-based education. State organization and activities can both reflect and direct what districts and schools need to do to help students learn

at the high levels being held out to them.

States also have a serious and challenging role vis-à-vis students. Many educators in many states do not believe that all students can achieve high levels of knowledge, skill, and performance. States must make it clear that not only is it possible for students to attain high standards, but that students have the right to the chance to show they can. In this role, the states become advocates, pressing for the education children need and deserve. States must model and promote the idea that a successful education is the result of schools being ready to serve all students, not just those "ready for school."

State education policy can make advocacy a reality, focusing on high goals for children and avoiding programs that segregate students on the basis of supposed differences in aptitude or condition. This is especially important in the arts, where all too often only gifted and talented students, or students fortunate enough to live in a relatively affluent school district, have access to a rich education in the arts. Such an education should be available to all students. To achieve this end, states must not simply see to it that the appropriate materials and resources are available. They must also support preservice education and professional development that gives both classroom teachers and specialists the knowledge and skills to deliver a rich curriculum in the arts.

States can also lead by demanding that districts be accountable for achieving each state's adopted standards. Like the standards themselves, the forms of accountability should be comprehensive. In the arts, these might include performance assessments, students portfolios, the conditions of learning, learning resources and technology, and the capabilities of teachers. Kentucky, for example, has included on its state arts assessment an item that asks students to describe and compare three dance forms, discussing how each form and its music reflect the traditions and customs of different societies. Challenging accountability mechanisms can also help ensure that students have the resources necessary for learning. If, for example, a state assessment requires students to create pictures with crayons, paints, or colored chalk, schools should be held accountable for providing access to these resources, just as they would be if the requirement were for students to use calculators in a mathematics course.

Technical Assistance. Local schools and districts will need considerable assistance in implementing the standards, and they will naturally and rightly look to the states for help. Just as the standards will challenge students in new ways, so they will challenge teachers, demanding new approaches to professional and preprofessional development. Pulling teachers together for one or two days of information sessions and workshops, loading them with unrelated—and sometimes irrelevant—materials, and layering new demands on top of old requirements has not been a successful reform strategy in the past. Nor will it produce the rich expertise teachers will

now need in a more demanding pedagogical environment. Above all, teachers need time to deal with the content and skills delineated by new national standards. That time will necessarily stretch out over months and years. Creating it will require creative management, new models of professional development, and perhaps even finding ways to reconfigure the school day and year.

New teachers graduating from teacher preparation programs should present, as part of the requirements for licensure, evidence that they have the knowledge, skills, and dispositions that are at least equal to those demanded of their students. They should present evidence that they are disposed to continually develop their skills and expertise, both in content areas and in pedagogy.

Technology offers an avenue for professional development and the thoughtful sharing of ideas among teachers. One way states can help teachers and their districts is by establishing electronic networks and bulletin boards for information and sharing resources. States can also help broker the resources necessary for teachers and students to have access to technology in their classrooms. This assistance is especially important to arts instruction because a wide range of technologies, from audiotapes to video laser disks, can be used to address so many elements of arts education. Technology also offers effective ways to help students learn a wide range of content and skills. For example, simulation activities or technology-based projects require students to learn and apply diverse skills and knowledge across content areas in realistic and challenging ways.

Barriers to Implementation

Prejudices. As states move toward implementation, barriers will naturally arise. One that is sure to come up for the arts Standards is the prevailing prejudice that some students are incapable of high levels of achievement and that especially gifted students are the only ones who can benefit from a rigorous arts education. This view is particularly difficult to root out because so many who hold it are unaware of their own biases. States will therefore need to work all the harder to address this dual misconception as they bring their policies and programs into sharper focus.

◆

States will need not only to develop new programs but also to revise, realign, and replace existing ones.

◆

A further prejudice considers some content areas, such as the arts, as frills and insists that the majority of students do not need challenging content in these areas. This view, too, will have to be combatted, especially because it is too easily adopted when competition over scarce resources emerges at the local level.

Contradictory Policies and Programs. Another barrier to using standards as a lever for statewide educational reform is programs and policies that are inconsistent with the new educational vision that standards help us see. These contradictory efforts are often difficult to change or replace. For example, students who are pulled out of class for special programs often lose access to important learning and are ultimately hampered by the very programs designed to help them. States will need not only to develop new programs but also to revise, realign, and replace existing ones. Faced with such problems, state staffs cannot afford to operate in a territorial way; they have to be able to cooperate if the standards are to do their job for children.

Oversimplification. A further barrier is the tendency to oversimplify. In an effort to make standards easier to understand and implement, states may be tempted to take what are truly complex visions for education and turn them into simple, misconstrued—and therefore misapplied—guidelines. Such a problem could easily take the form of an overemphasis on some standards at the expense of others, or the temptation to try to make effective only those standards that address basic skills. If the standards are interpreted in a way that makes it impossible for them to hold out challenging learning goals to students, they will not provide the impetus for better learning or better teaching.

A State Responsibility

The role of the states in implementing national education standards is crucial. Because states have the constitutional responsibility for educating our children, they must be the major source of information, coordination, advocacy and leadership, and technical assistance to local school districts and schools. The complexity of the national standards increases the need for challenge of their role. States can support one another and seek assistance from national groups such as the Council of Chief State School Officers, the U.S. Department of Education, and the several professional associations serving teachers in the academic disciplines. But ultimately the responsibility rests with the states.

States already understand that substantive change requires a coordinated effort in how we go about educating students. They also understand that the buck stops with them. With a clear vision of education goals sharpened by new and more challenging academic standards, with coordinated efforts to reach refocused goals, and with the right allocation of time, energy, and resources, states should be able to make the right changes for students to attain the high levels of achievement held out by the standards.

Barbara Kapinus, **Frank Philip**, **Jon Quam**, and **Ramsay Selden** are members of the staff of the Council of Chief State School Officers in Washington, D.C. **Alan Morgan** is the president of the Council and the state superintendent of public instruction in New Mexico.

Working with State Legislatures

Louise Miller

It is unlikely that many elected officials are aware of the project to develop and implement the National Standards for Arts Education, whether they work as policymakers at the national, state, or local level. Most elected officials are still operating on the assumption that we are a "nation at risk," working to reform our schools so that we spend more money, train better teachers, beef up technology, and test our students more frequently in reading, writing, math, and science. The focus in our K–12 systems is on a "back-to-basics" philosophy. The arts have been and sometimes still are viewed as nonacademic, elective, or extra-curricular.

In the late 1980s, my own state of Washington found that, as in most of the rest of the nation, basic arts education did not exist. In many school districts, students had no arts courses after leaving elementary school. Developing a strategy for implementing the Standards will require ensuring that states, which have the constitutional responsibility for education, understand first what is at stake for our children's education and why the arts must be included as a part of the core curriculum. And that means working with the state legislators who pass the laws that guide the policy process.

What Legislators Need and Can Do

The fact that the arts are presented as core subjects in the Goals 2000: Educate America Act is a sign of significant progress. But a national law does not get the state's job done. Legislators now need more information documenting the importance and value of an education in the arts for every student. Particularly persuasive for them will be the research data showing that students from all backgrounds who study the arts do better in other academic areas, stay in school, attend school regularly, work well with others, think creatively and critically, and are enthusiastic and motivated about school. Legislators also need better information about the economics of the arts for their states. For example, they need to know that corporate America is learning that students who have studied the arts make better employees.

Legislators and their staff members will need to visit schools in their own districts that have already started integrating the arts deeper into the curriculum. A few special-interest groups who advocate and work to implement the Standards are no guarantee of a national strategy, nor do they guarantee that states will automatically adopt the arts as basic. For that to happen, legislators in every state need to have ownership of the idea and make it one of their personal priorities. This ownership means, in turn, that legislators who already understand the value of the arts for education have a role to play in convincing their colleagues.

One way that support, information, and coordination in this task can be achieved is through the National Conference of State Legislatures (NCSL).

◆

Legislators who already understand the value of the arts for education have a role to play in convincing their colleagues.

◆

Working through NCSL's committee structure, key state legislators can present a resolution at the NCSL summer meeting to include arts education in the basic K–12 curriculum in all the member states. An adopted resolution would ensure a national focus on putting and keeping the arts on the agenda for new education guidelines throughout the country.

Building State Strategies: The First Step

About half the states have already adopted an education code or resolution that supports making the arts part of the basic curriculum. For a state legislator whose state has not adopted language in state law to include arts as part of the basic K–12 curriculum, seeking that change is a first job. Each state legislature will need groups of citizens to support the effort and fuel grass-roots activities. Included in the lobbying cadre should be teacher, parent, business, and student organizations; arts organizations that can lend support include local and state arts alliances, professional performing groups and individuals, visual artists, community and corporate arts councils, and others who will work to secure passage of the appropriate legislation.

Passing the Implementation Bill. The legislature's first step is to find a credible sponsor or set of sponsors for the bill, which should be introduced in both houses of the legislature with bipartisan support. In Washington, our legislature's Education Reform Bill was the best vehicle for including the arts as part of basic education; in some states a separate piece of legislation may be necessary. Most legislatures have an education committee in one or both houses; the best bill-sponsors would be the chair, vice-chair, and ranking minority members of that committee. The inner politics of each legislature will decide which house's bill eventually makes it to the governor's desk.

Support by advocates and experts will have to be carefully orchestrated through testimony at appropriate hearings. Legislative and committee staff can help with keeping phone calls, visits to the state capitol, and letter-writing efforts timed to the legislative schedule.

Volunteer advocates need to understand that a personal contact with all legislators is a must. Constituents, or second best, people outside their districts who know legislators personally, are the best representatives. Citizens who are not familiar with the lobbying process need to know that timing is crucial. Also, computer-generated or duplicated letters are not very effective, and personal phone calls are better than toll-free hotlines. Handwritten postcards or letters to their own legislator are every citizen's best bet for registering views and expressing opinions.

Everyone needs to understand that they are in for the long haul. A bill can go through two or three committees in each house of the legislature, with many changes along the way, before it reaches the governor's desk. Support groups have to be well prepared for the final

stage, which could include a separate lobbying effort to make sure the governor does not veto the bill. Key sponsors in the governor's own party, or legislators who have a good working relationship with the executive, can help forestall a veto.

In many legislatures, the executive review of bills happens after the legislative session has adjourned. This means that someone needs to track the bill's progress through the governor's office. Prime sponsors may be able to do this, but very often, especially in part-time legislatures, elected members have other jobs and lack the support staff to track the bill. The bill can be lost in this final stage for the entire year or in some cases for the biennium. The long haul requires the kind of vigilance that keeps supporters in line long enough to see the legislation all the way through.

The Next Step: Making Policy Real

Once the arts education requirement is on the statute books, the next step is defining the steps needed to make the policy a reality. Most states have boards of education and some have education departments, but in most legislative bodies the working relationships that matter most for implementing education policies are with the state school superintendent, the state school board president and the executive directors of the state school board association, the state teachers organization(s), and in some cases, the president or legislative chair of the state Parent Teacher Association (PTA).

WORKING WITH STATE LEGISLATURES

All these organizations and individuals need to be involved in the next phase of the legislative agenda. This may include everything from bills for capital funding for buildings and equipment, to money for hiring teaching specialists, to additional appropriations that will assure professional development in arts education and more comprehensive teacher preparation. Many who have already worked on the Standards have pointed out that the most difficult task will be providing resources, and most especially, developing new training methods for classroom teachers. Most states will have to pass new legislation to meet these needs.

It may seem important to have the legislature prescribe the details about curriculum, instructional time, professional development, and the like. In fact, it is more important to get a clear idea of what will be achieved by including arts in the basic graduation requirement, to make an estimate of the funding needed to implement the Standards, and to know how frequently students will need to be assessed. Details about instructional time, specialized teachers, facilities, materials, and other factors involved in implementing the Standards should be left to local school districts and educational professionals. Policy guidelines should allow maximum flexibility while still setting definite state educational goals.

Such would be the case, for example, in the crucial task of retooling teacher preparation institutions to produce the teachers the new arts Standards will

require, and the kind of certification needed. That task is examined next.

Teacher Preparation. After completing a preliminary study, legislators would work to draft a bill that addresses the implementation role of higher educa-

◆

If the [legislator] can't come to the schools to observe what is happening in arts education programs, advocates have to be ready to take the schools to them.

◆

tion institutions. Almost every state has an appointed, cabinet-level organization, such as a board of higher education, that would play a role in crafting the needed legislation and lead the lobbying effort for the bill. If the initiative comes from the executive, it will almost automatically ensure that the prime sponsors are some of the top legislators in the majority party. The bill, or package of bills, goes through the process described already. The main difference is that now the power and legislative expertise of the governor and his or her staff will be leading the effort for passage. This will likely improve the bill's chances, but because there is no sure thing in politics, vigilance is again required.

Some Final Suggestions. Legislators, like everyone else, like to be able to tell success stories. When it comes to implementing the arts Standards, successes in the neighborhood schools in their own districts are the best kind. If the member can't come to the schools to observe what is happening in arts education programs, advocates have to be ready to take the schools to them. Most effective will be a class of young students, their teacher, and a parent-helper who go to the legislator's office to demonstrate that the integrated learning, skills, knowledge, and use of the arts can be an enlivening experience, even to an uninformed observer.

There are many challenges in implementing the Standards. Legislators—and those who vote for them—have a critical role to play. If they are to do their jobs well, legislators must be well informed, and those who want to make implementation a reality need a thorough understanding of how to "work" the legislative process. Advocates who know how to make legislators' work easier, both by providing good information and by doing the groundwork to make a vote for the arts an attractive one, will, in the end, be doing the best possible job of implementing the Standards.

Louise Miller is a former state legislator and currently serves as a member of the Metropolitan King County (Washington) Council.

Where We Go from Here
A Strategic Summary

Despite the diversity of perspectives and the wide range of ideas presented in these essays, the authors display an impressive unanimity of spirit. They are in agreement, for example, that the National Standards for Arts Education are a historic development. Several point out that, for the first time in the history of education in the United States, the arts have a place at the core of academic study in our schools. There is also for the first time broad agreement on what young people ought to know and be able to do in the arts, and when. But the authors are likewise agreed that a short public attention span and relentless competition for shrinking education dollars will require arts educators to work hard to keep what has been accomplished thus far.

There is consensus that implementing the Standards at the state, district, building, and classroom levels—that is, making them a part of both education policy and the delivery of education services—will be no easy job. It will require a coalition-building effort the likes of which we have not yet seen in arts education in this country. That effort will require all stakeholders to become active participants. The critical members of this stakeholder group, as noted in the strategy articles, include parents, teachers, school administrators, legislators and education policy makers at all levels, business and community leaders, and the arts community—including arts alliances, professional associations of arts educators, and individual artists.

But these articles offer more than recognition of a historic moment or a list of people and the jobs each must do. They also sketch, in broad strokes, the outline of a strategic vision. They are firm in their insistence that the keys to overall success in implementing the Standards will include—at the very least—working to create the following:

♦ A strong program of information and advocacy at all levels, but especially at the local level, both to raise public awareness about the value and benefits of arts education and to win public support for the Standards, and a concomitant commitment to a strategic approach organized from the bottom up.

◆ A clear understanding that implementation of the Standards is a matter of devising, at all levels, a policy framework. That means declaring that the Standards are part of a clear understanding of what is meant by "education" and of a commitment to standards as a part of how we educate. That means, in turn, that the Standards are part of a political process, in which decision makers at all levels must be contacted, informed, and persuaded to adopt and implement the Standards.

◆ A broad-based commitment to institute and improve programs of professional development and teacher preparation, both to support implementation of the Standards and to improve arts education.

◆ Quick construction of the mechanisms that can assure appropriate assessment, local accountability, local coordination, and the responsible use of interdisciplinary education.

◆ The personnel and material resources to ensure the equity of arts programming and an educational infrastructure adequate to a sound education in the arts, at all levels of instruction.

A National Campaign Strategy

These essays offer, in effect, the first draft of a national campaign strategy to implement the new Standards. But these authors are still feeling their way. Much

has yet to be learned, and most of that learning will be in the doing. Whether discussing issues or strategies, the authors do not say exactly, step by step, how things should be done. But that is, for them, no reason to suspend operations until we have more clarity. They would have much sympathy, I believe, with the advice of President Franklin D. Roosevelt, who noted in a 1932 address that "the country needs, and, unless I mistake its temper, demands, bold experimentation. It is common sense to take a method and try it. If it fails, admit it frankly and try another. But above all, try something."

These articles are realistic in recognizing that local conditions require flexibility, not a cookbook approach. Many details are lacking; in many places the concerns of the authors overlap. But nothing important has been left out. The journey will be a long one. There will be changes of direction, new thinking, and new challenges. Each state will move to meet its own needs in its own way, but Cawelti is right to insist that the policy issue is paramount; states will have to declare themselves on what they intend to do about arts education. But with what is here, the journey toward a comprehensive, sequential arts education for every child can now get under way.

What follows sums up the strategic efforts that must engage the attention of different stakeholder groups, organized according to the points noted in the bulleted section above. The constituency groups engaged by the strategy articles will see, readily enough, where they can make their own contributions. They are encouraged to consult the individual articles for more details.

Information and Advocacy. Advocacy lies at the core of implementation because it is the royal road to decision makers. It is also the lifeblood of the policy process. Those with a strong role to play, as several authors note, are parents, teachers, school board members, legislators, and the public. Implementing the Standards, the writers argue, will be impossible without giving decision makers the information they need about why an arts education is important and how the Standards make it possible to deliver one. As both Bruhn and Lynch note, a key ingredient for success on this front is to deliver clear and consistent messages about the importance of the Standards. The national information networks of all these groups are powerful resources for recruiting advocates, interpreting the Standards themselves, and persuading decision makers to act. But these authors are also agreed that the information and advocacy task must be strongest at the local level. Here is where energy and support must be garnered; a "top-down" approach will not work.

The Policy Process and Coalition Building. The policy process is about three things: declaring what is important (information and advocacy), gaining support (coalition building), and eventually, allocating resources to achieve goals (decision making). Real power, as Bruhn, Miller, Johnson, Waikart, and Canada point out most forcefully, comes from touching the soil at the local level.

Everyone who has a stake there has a role to play, whether as a member of a formally organized group, or simply by virtue of his or her position or responsibility.

If the "from the grass roots up" perspective that most of these authors reflect is to bear fruit, the role of parents (read: taxpaying citizens) in building local and state coalitions will be critical. Although no one will organize the parents, their support from a political point of view is essential, because the Standards are not likely to see implementation without them. But their effort can be magnified many times over by their natural allies in local and state coalitions: PTAs, national associations of teachers in the arts disciplines, local and state arts alliances, as well as local arts groups. Because their diversity and energy are impressive to decision makers, coalitions comprising such groups can make a profound impact on the policy process. Among the most important of these stakeholder groups, as Gurin argues, is the local business community. It has a bottom-line stake in what arts education can provide to the future work force, and business people can often acquire the ear of decision makers when others cannot.

The local school administrator, working as a servant of the local school board, has the responsibility for putting flesh on the policy bones. Many, as Canada points out, lack the training and background in arts education to act on their own to effect implementation, which is why their alliances with parents and teachers are so crucial. But their position in the policy process has strategic value. Situated halfway between parents and teachers seeking change, and state officials who guard the public purse, school administrators (and their state and national professional organizations) can take an active role in lobbying state legislatures for the resources needed to implement the Standards and to develop new curricular frameworks.

The role of local school boards vis-à-vis the Standards, as Johnson points out, is to shape local thinking and lead parents and community members to understand that the arts are a basic part of the curriculum, not by administrative fiat but by persuading skeptics that the arts are intrinsic to what it means to be an educated human being. In particular, school boards will be called on, with state education agencies and higher education institutions, to address two of the most formidable barriers to implementation: the need for resources and professional development. In particular, it will fall to local school boards to wrestle with how to find teachers the time, perhaps by restructuring the school schedule, to learn and grow into the new responsibilities and skills the Standards will require.

At the state education agency level, the policy process crystallizes into the four major functions noted by Kapinus et. al.: information, coordination, advocacy, and leadership. The major support for local school districts trying to implement the Standards will need to come from the states, in the form of models, curricular frameworks, and professional

development initiatives. States should make it clear as a matter of policy not only that achieving the arts education Standards is possible for all students, but also that the opportunity to do so is each student's right. States can also lead by demanding accountability from local districts for achieving the Standards, recognizing that their moral grounding for doing so is their covenant with those who provide the resources to educate all our children.

The final link in the policy chain is the state legislature. With the state executive, they decide on the overarching legal framework for the place of the arts in the curriculum. Unless the legislature's decision-making process is informed by coalition builders, the temptation to follow the path of least political resistance is great. Legislatures will also be the most important groups deciding about the additional resources needed to implement all the academic standards being written by various subject-area groups. It is up to advocates to make sure that decisions are made in the light of questions such as "What kind of education do we want our children to have?" and are not driven entirely by "How thinly can the existing pie be sliced?"

Legislatures, as Miller notes, are not beyond reach of local efforts just because they meet in the state capitol. Each individual legislator is the knot in the rope that binds the policy process to some local group or coalition, because what legislatures are all about, in the end, is what voters say they want government to do. In other words, the temptation to construe implementation of the Standards as strictly an educational issue is misguided. It is every bit as political as it is pedagogical; it is about both vision and votes. It is therefore crucial, as several authors point out, that local legislators be a focus for every coalition-building effort.

Professional Development and Teacher Preparation. The essays in this collection speak with one voice on this issue. No other effort more directly affects the success of Standards implementation where it counts—in the classroom—than professional development and teacher preparation. Included in this part of the strategy, as Hoffa points out, are the changes that will have to be made in teacher credentialing and degree requirements, teacher-preparation curricula, continuing education and in-service models for teachers, and in-service education delivery. State education agencies, institutions of higher education, local school boards, and administrators are all involved in making decisions about these matters. They represent a powerful community of interest. Among the most helpful resources in making the needed changes in all these arenas will be the national professional associations for teachers in the arts disciplines. Altogether, that is a formidable community of interest. If we are to develop the teaching force needed to implement the Standards, attention to professional development must be unremitting; here is where all who care about arts education need to be in it for the long term.

Mechanisms for Implementing the

Standards. The Standards cannot be implemented well unless mechanisms are in place for delivering appropriate assessment, local accountability, and the responsible use of interdisciplinary education. The Standards themselves promise to provide assistance in all these areas, for they bring order to many areas where it has been lacking.

Assessment in the arts, for example, has always been complex. New assessment models appropriate to each arts discipline—that is, a catalogue of assessment strategies for identifying levels of student achievement, as well as across a range of different time periods and kinds of activities—can be adopted district by district, with assistance from state education agencies. Of particular value, as Lehman notes, will be assessment strategies related to analyzing, describing, and evaluating works of art; these are less well developed in the arts than assessment models for creating and performing. Among the most far-reaching, but not yet widely discussed, impacts of the Standards on assessment will be the boost they give to alternative forms of student assessment across the board. Once again, the immediate strategic task has a long-range dimension.

Strong structures of accountability do not yet exist for arts education at the local level. These structures will, of course, follow existing lines of authority. State legislatures, state education agencies, and other sources of funds and resources for implementation—particularly those associated with teacher preparation and professional development—will insist on accountability in return for the support they provide to arts education. The use of interdisciplinary education approaches and models is, potentially, among the most potent resources arts education has to offer to the improvement of teaching and the general curriculum. But, as Hope points out vigorously, the greatest danger accompanying that strategy is superficiality.

Equity. The implementation of standards in all academic areas will have serious, systemwide implications on the implementation of the arts Standards, largely by intensifying the competition for scarce educational resources. Arts education advocates will need to become more, not less, heavily involved in equity issues, now that the arts have been included among the core academic subjects. Fehrs-Rampolla and Canada are right to insist that teachers, school systems, and policymakers will all have to address questions of how resources and opportunities (programs, teachers, materials, and most often neglected, time) will

be allocated to assure that *all* children receive an education in the arts commensurate with the quality the Standards point toward.

From "Well Begun..." to "Well Done!"

Successful implementation of the Standards will not just happen. If it is to happen, the best time to begin is now to bring the attainment of the Standards within the reach of every child.

The arts have much to contribute to the education and lives of America's children. The National Standards for Arts Education offer them an opportunity to achieve much, to expand their horizons, to explore new meanings, and to acquire a way of understanding the world, and their experience of it, that is invaluable. Having created these Standards, the temptation to rest on a bed of laurels must be resisted. We know what we must do. That task will not be easy, nor will it be accomplished soon. But it is a task already well begun. What remains, for all of us, is to see it well done. —BB

APPENDIX A: WHERE YOU CAN GET HELP

Print Publications

America's Culture Begins with Education. Reston, VA: Music Educators National Conference, 1990.

Arts Education Partnership Working Group. *The Power of the Arts to Transform Education.* Washington, DC: The John F. Kennedy Center for the Performing Arts, 1993.

Arts for Everykid: A Handbook for Change. Trenton, NJ: New Jersey State Council on the Arts/Alliance for Arts Education, 1992.

Arts for Living. Washington, DC: National Committee on Arts for the Handicapped, 1985.

Arts in Schools: Perspectives from Four Nations. Washington, DC: National Endowment for the Arts, 1993.

Fowler, Charles. *Can We Rescue the Arts for America's Children?* New York: American Council for the Arts, 1988.

Gardner, Howard. *Frames of Mind: The Theory of Multiple Intelligences.* New York: Basic Books, 1983.

Katz, Jonathan, ed. *Arts & Education Handbook: A Guide to Productive Collaborations.* Washington, DC: National Assembly of State Arts Agencies, 1988.

Making Sense of School Budgets. Washington, DC: U.S. Department of Education, Office of Educational Research and Improvement, 1989.

More Than Pumpkins in October: Visual Literacy in the 21st Century (kit). Los Angeles: Getty Center for Education in the Arts, 1992.

Murfree, Elizabeth. *The Value of the Arts.* Washington, DC: President's Committee on the Arts and the Humanities, 1992.

National Coalition for Music Education. *Action Kit for Music Education.* Reston, VA: Music Educators National Conference, 1991.

National Coalition for Music Education. *Building Support for School Music: A Practical Guide.* Reston, VA: Music Educators National Conference, 1991.

National Coalition for Music Education. *Growing Up Complete: The Imperative for Music Education.* Reston, VA: Music Educators National Conference, 1991.

National Coalition for Music Education. *Teacher's Guide for Advocacy.* Reston, VA: Music Educators National Conference, 1992.

National PTA. *Be Smart, Include Art: A Planning Kit for PTAs.* Los Angeles: Getty Center for Education in the Arts, 1992.

National PTA. *Make Art a Part of Your Child's World.* Los Angeles: Getty Center for Education in the Arts, 1992.

National Standards for Arts Education: What Every Young American Should Know and Be Able to Do in the Arts. Reston, VA: Music Educators National Conference, 1994.

Nuts and Bolts #3: Coalitions—Joining Them, Building Them, and Making Them Work. Chicago: The National PTA, 1992.

Nuts and Bolts #6: How to Conduct a Reflections Program. Chicago: The National PTA, 1992.

Organization and Management Group, with Charles Fowler and Bernard J. McMullan. *Understanding How the Arts Contribute to Excellent Education.* Washington, DC: National Endowment for the Arts, 1991.

Performing Together: The Arts and Education. Arlington, VA: American Association of School Administrators, 1985.

Perspective: The Arts and School Reform. Washington, DC: Council for Basic Education, 1993.

Perspectives on Education Reform: Arts Education as Catalyst. Los Angeles: Getty Center for Education in the Arts, 1993.

Promoting School Art. Reston, VA: National Art Education Association, 1987.

Quality Art Education: Goals for Schools. Reston, VA: National Art Education Association, 1986.

Reinventing the Wheel: A Design for Student Achievement in the 21st Century. Denver: National Conference of State Legislatures, 1992.

Remer, Jane. *Changing Schools through the Arts: How to Build on the Power of an Idea.* New York: American Council for the Arts, 1990.

School Is What WE Make It! A Parent Involvement Planning Kit. Chicago: The National PTA, 1993.

Toward Civilization: A Report on Arts Education. Washington, DC: National Endowment for the Arts, 1988.

The Vision for Arts Education in the 21st Century. Reston, VA: Music Educators National Conference, 1994.

What Work Requires of Schools: A SCANS Report for America 2000. Washington, DC: U.S. Department of Labor, 1991.

Why Business Should Support the Arts: Facts, Figures, and Philosophy. New York: Business Committee for the Arts, 1991.

Why We Need the Arts. New York: American Council for the Arts, 1989.

Williams, Harold M. *The Language of Civilization: The Vital Role of the Arts in Education.* Washington, DC: President's Committee on the Arts and Humanities, 1991.

Videotapes

The Art of Learning. Los Angeles: Getty Center for Education in the Arts, 1993.

Arts for Life. Los Angeles: Getty Center for Education in the Arts, 1990.

Arts in America. Washington, DC: National Endowment for the Arts, 1992.

Benham, John. *School Music and "Reverse Economics."* Reston, VA: Music Educators National Conference, 1991.

"Broken Arts," in the *Learning Matters* series. New York: American Community Service Network and South Carolina Educational Television, 1993. (800-277-0829)

The Imagination Machines. Los Angeles: Getty Center for Education in the Arts, 1991.

Lautzenheiser, Tim, and Henry Mancini. *Let's Make Music/A Way of Learning.* Reston, VA: Music Educators National Conference, 1991.

The Value of Art in Education. Los Angeles: Getty Center for Education in the Arts, 1988.

Education Reform, Standards, and the Arts

This statement briefly spells out the goals of the Standards and describes the context from which they emerged. Readers are encouraged to duplicate this summary for distribution to all those who can help implement the Standards.

These National Standards for Arts Education are a statement of what every young American should know and be able to do in four arts disciplines— dance, music, theatre, and the visual arts. Their scope is grades K–12, and they speak to both content and achievement.

The Reform Context. The Standards are one outcome of the education reform effort generated in the 1980s, which emerged in several states and attained nationwide visibility with the publication of *A Nation at Risk* in 1983. This national wake-up call was powerfully effective. Six national education goals were announced in 1990. Now there is a broad effort to describe, specifically, the knowledge and skills students must have in all subjects to fulfill their personal potential, to become productive and competitive workers in a global economy, and to take their places as adult citizens. With the passage of the Goals 2000: Educate America Act, the national goals are written into law, naming the arts as a core, academic subject—as important to education as English, mathematics, history, civics and government, geography, science, and foreign language.

At the same time, the Act calls for education standards in these subject areas, both to encourage high achievement by our young people and to provide benchmarks to determine how well they are learning and performing. In 1992, anticipating that education standards would emerge as a focal point of the reform legislation, the Consortium of National Arts Education Associations successfully approached the U.S. Department of Education, the National Endowment for the Arts, and the

111

National Endowment for the Humanities for a grant to determine what the nation's school children should know and be able to do in the arts. This document is the result of an extended process of consensus-building that drew on the broadest possible range of expertise and participation. The process involved the review of state-level arts education frameworks, standards from other nations, and consideration at a series of national forums.

The Importance of Standards. Agreement on what students should know and be able to do is essential if education is to be consistent, efficient, and effective. In this context, Standards for arts education are important for two basic reasons. First, they help define what a good education in the arts should provide: a thorough grounding in a basic body of knowledge and the skills required both to make sense and make use of the arts disciplines. Second, when states and school districts adopt these Standards, they are taking a stand for rigor in a part of education that has too often, and wrongly, been treated as optional. This document says, in effect, "an education in the arts means that students should know what is spelled out here, and they should reach clear levels of attainment at these grade levels."

These Standards provide a vision of competence and educational effectiveness, but without creating a mold into which all arts programs must fit. The Standards are concerned with the *results* (in the form of student learning) that come from a basic education in the arts, *not with how those results ought to be delivered.* Those matters are for states, localities, and classroom teachers to decide. In other words, while the Standards provide educational goals and not a curriculum, they can help improve all types of arts instruction.

The Importance of Arts Education. Knowing and practicing the arts disciplines are fundamental to the healthy development of children's minds and spirits. That is why, in any civilization— ours included—the arts are inseparable from the very meaning of the term "education." We know from long experience that no one can claim to be truly educated who lacks basic knowledge and skills in the arts. There are many reasons for this assertion:

♦ The arts are worth studying simply because of what they are. Their impact cannot be denied. Throughout history, all the arts have served to connect our imaginations with the deepest questions of human existence: Who am I? What must I do? Where am I going? Studying responses to those questions through time and across cultures— as well as acquiring the tools and knowledge to create one's own responses—is essential not only to understanding life but to living it fully.

♦ The arts are used to achieve a multitude of human purposes: to present issues and ideas, to teach or persuade, to entertain, to decorate or please. Becoming literate in the arts helps students understand and do these things better.

♦ The arts are integral to every person's daily life. Our personal, social, economic, and cultural environments are shaped by the arts at every turn—from the design of the child's breakfast placemat, to the songs on the commuter's car radio, to the family's nighttime TV drama, to the teenager's Saturday dance, to the enduring influences of the classics.

♦ The arts offer unique sources of enjoyment and refreshment for the imagination. They explore relationships between ideas and objects and serve as links between thought and action. Their continuing gift is to help us see and grasp life in new ways.

♦ There is ample evidence that the arts help students develop the attitudes, characteristics, and intellectual skills required to participate effectively in today's society and economy. The arts teach self-discipline, reinforce self-esteem, and foster the thinking skills and creativity so valued in the workplace. They teach the importance of teamwork and cooperation. They demonstrate the direct connection between study, hard work, and high levels of achievement.

The Benefits of Arts Education. Arts education benefits the *student* because it cultivates the whole child, gradually building many kinds of literacy while developing intuition, reasoning, imagination, and dexterity into unique forms of expression and communication. This process requires not merely an active mind but a trained one. An education in the arts benefits *society* because students of the arts gain powerful tools for understanding human experiences, both past and present. They learn to respect the often very different ways others have of thinking, working, and expressing themselves. They learn to make decisions in situations where there are no standard answers. By studying the arts, students stimulate their natural creativity and learn to develop it to meet the needs of a complex and competitive society. And, as study and competence in the arts reinforce one other, the joy of learning becomes real, tangible, and powerful.

The Arts and Other Core Subjects. The Standards address competence in the arts disciplines first of all. But that competence provides a firm foundation for connecting arts-related concepts and facts across the art forms, and from them to the sciences and humanities. For example, the intellectual methods of the arts are precisely those used to transform scientific disciplines and discoveries into everyday technology.

What Must We Do? The educational success of our children depends on creating a society that is both literate and imaginative, both competent and creative. That goal depends, in turn, on providing children with tools not only for understanding that world but for contributing to it and making their own way. Without the arts to help shape students' perceptions and imaginations, our children stand every chance of growing into adulthood as culturally disabled. We must not allow that to happen.

Without question, the Standards presented here will need supporters and allies to improve how arts education is organized and delivered. They have the potential to change education policy at all levels, and to make a transforming impact across the entire spectrum of education.

But only if they are implemented.

Teachers, of course, will be the leaders in this process. In many places, more teachers with credentials in the arts, as well as better-trained teachers in general, will be needed. Site-based management teams, school boards, state education agencies, state and local arts agencies, and teacher education institutions will all have a part to play, as will local

mentors, artists, local arts organizations, and members of the community. Their support is crucial for the Standards to succeed. But the primary issue is the ability to bring together and deliver a broad range of competent instruction. All else is secondary.

In the end, truly successful implementation can come about only when students and their learning are at the center, which means motivating and enabling them to meet the Standards. With a steady gaze on that target, these Standards can empower America's schools to make changes consistent with the best any of us can envision, for our children and for our society.

Reprinted from *National Standards for Arts Education: What Every Young American Should Know and Be Able to Do in the Arts,* developed by the Consortium of National Arts Education Associations. Reston, VA: Music Educators National Conference, 1994.

Consultants to the Implementation Task Force

Gordon Cawelti currently serves as the executive director of the Alliance for Curriculum Reform, a newly formed alliance of the twenty-five major subject-matter groups that have organized to accelerate curriculum reform in the United States. In his previous position, he was the executive director of the Association for Supervision and Curriculum Development (1973–1992). He serves on a large number of advisory boards and has received many recognitions of his contributions to education.

A. Graham Down is the president of the Council for Basic Education. He served as chair of the National Committee for Standards in the Arts and as cochair of the Steering Committee to develop a framework for the projected assessment of arts education in the 1996 National Assessment of Educational Progress. Down is currently the organist and director of music at Western Presbyterian Church in Washington, D.C. He is president of the popular "Music at Noon" concert series, and he serves on the boards of directors of the National Foundation for Advancement in the Arts and the Washington Bach Consort.

Implementation Task Force

Karl Bruhn recently retired as director for market development of the National Association of Music Merchants (NAMM), where he helped found the National Coalition for Music Education, which involves teachers, parents, and school administrators across the country in advocacy for music education. Before joining NAMM, he served as senior vice-president for marketing with the Yamaha Corporation of America. In recognition of his advocacy efforts, Bruhn was awarded an honorary Doctor of Music degree by the Berklee College of Music in 1993. An accomplished musician, he played professionally and led his own orchestra for many years.

Benjamin O. Canada is the superintendent of the Jackson (Mississippi) Public School District. He was the deputy superintendent of schools in Tucson, Arizona, from 1988 to 1990 and the assistant superintendent for business and operations services there from 1986 to 1987. Canada has been an elementary, junior high, and high school principal and has served on the board of directors of the Mississippi Symphony and on the advisory board of the Mississippi Association of Talented and Gifted.

Barbara Fehrs-Rampolla is an art teacher at Holmdel High School in New Jersey and a ceramicist. Fehrs-Rampolla is currently working as a member of the Educational Testing Service test development committee for the Praxis II Subject Assessment in Visual Art. She also serves as the coordinator of the Artist/Educator Initiative for the Geraldine R. Dodge Foundation. As the 1989 recipient of a New Jersey Governor's Teacher Grant, Fehrs-Rampolla completed a project titled

"Accepting Diversity: A Multicultural Arts Approach."

Richard S. Gurin has been president and chief executive officer of Binney & Smith, Inc., makers of Crayola and Liquitex brand art products, since 1987. In 1990, he was appointed to the board of the American Council for the Arts in New York City and currently serves as a vice-chairman. In December 1992, he was appointed chairman of the Advisory Council on Arts Education at the National Endowment for the Arts. In 1993, he was named to the National Cultural Alliance Leadership Council and the America 2000 Coalition Board of Directors.

Harlan Edward Hoffa is an art educator who held academic and administrative appointments at Pennsylvania State University from 1970 until his retirement in 1990. Before that, he taught at Indiana, Boston, and Ohio State universities, at SUNY-Buffalo, and in the Evanston (Illinois) Public Schools. He served as president of the National Art Education Association from 1971 to 1973 and was the visual arts research specialist in the United States Office of Education's Arts and Humanities Program from 1964 to 1967. He is now an associate dean emeritus at Penn State.

Samuel Hope is the executive director of the National Associations of Schools of Art and Design, Schools of Dance, Schools of Music, and Schools of Theatre, the national accrediting agencies for collegiate-level programs that prepare arts professionals. Hope is an executive editor of *Arts Education Policy Review* and an editorial consultant for *The Journal of Aesthetic Education.* He holds degrees in composition from the Eastman School of Music and Yale University and is published regularly as a policy analyst and futurist in education, the arts, and accreditation.

Nancy Jo Johnson has been a member of the Dickinson (North Dakota) Public School District #1 Board of Education since 1984. She served as president from 1986 to 1989. From 1991 to 1993, Johnson served as vice-president/president-elect of the North Dakota School Boards Association and currently serves as its president. She was elected to the National School Boards Association's Board of Directors in 1992. Johnson is also a long-standing member and officer in the American Association of University Women.

Paul R. Lehman is professor of music and senior associate dean of the School of Music at the University of Michigan. He was president of the Music Educators National Conference (MENC) from 1984 to 1986. He has taught graduate courses in measurement and evaluation in music, and he is the author of a textbook on that topic. Since the 1960s, he has served on writing committees for the Advanced Placement examination in music, the NAEP assessments in music, the National Teacher Examination in music, and other projects in evaluation and assessment.

Robert L. Lynch has been president and chief executive officer of the National Assembly of Local Arts Agencies since 1985. Prior to that position, Lynch was the executive director of the Arts Extension Service (AES) of the Division of Continuing Education at the University of Massachusetts in Amherst. He played a leading role in the fight for more federal funds for the arts and for that funding to remain free of content restrictions. While at AES, he oversaw the development of a series of regional special projects designed to develop new audiences for the arts in rural and other areas.

Louise Miller serves on the Metropolitan King County Council and chairs its arts committee. From 1982 to 1993, she served in the Washington State Legislature; during that time, she also was a member of the Washington State Arts Commission and chaired a national arts and tourism committee of the National Council of State Legislatures. Prior to her experience as a legislator, Miller was a music teacher in Seattle.

Alan Morgan is the New Mexico state superintendent of public instruction. He has been with the New Mexico State Department of Education since 1972, and before that was an elementary school teacher. Morgan chaired the National Indicators Panel for the U.S. Congress in 1991–92 and is currently president of the Council of Chief State School Officers. He serves on approximately twenty state and national panels, boards, and commissions.

Kitty Waikart is chairman of the Cultural Arts Committee and a member of the Board of Directors of the National PTA. She served as state president for the South Carolina PTA from 1991 to 1993 and as Cultural Arts/Reflections chairman from 1986 to 1990. Waikart coordinated the South Carolina PTA pilot program for the development of the arts advocacy kit "Be Smart, Include Art," sponsored by the National PTA and the Getty Center for Education in the Arts. She has been active in the PTA at the local, state, and national levels for more than twenty years.

Project Editor

Bruce O. Boston is president of Wordsmith, a Washington, D.C.–based writing and editing consulting company. National reports he has helped write include *A Nation at Risk* (1983); *What Work Requires of Schools* and *Learning a Living*, the reports of the SCANS Commission of the U.S. Department of Labor (1991, 1992); *Growing Up Complete*, the report of the National Commission on Music Education (1991); and most recently, the *National Standards for Arts Education* (1994) and this book. He has published more than two hundred books and articles of his own and has edited several books.

Members of the Review Board

John S. Adams, chair, high school arts department, Hartford City, Indiana

Richard Bell, Young Audiences, Inc., New York, New York

Gretta Berghammer, chair, Department of Theatre, University of Northern Iowa, Cedar Falls, Iowa

Vicki S. Bodenhamer, Department of Public Instruction, Dover, Delaware

Carole Brandt, chair, Department of Theatre, Pennsylvania State University, University Park, Pennsylvania

Lillian M. Brinkley, elementary school principal, Norfolk, Virginia

Deborah Brzoska, fine arts administrator, Vancouver, Washington

Brian E. Curry, Association for Supervision and Curriculum Development, Alexandria, Virginia

James W. Eisenhardt, high school theatre teacher, Omaha, Nebraska

Kathryn G. Ellis, former high school dance teacher, Detroit, Michigan

Karl J. Glenn, high school music teacher, Detroit, Michigan

Mark Hansen, art resource coordinator, Forest Lake, Minnesota

Margaret Hilliard, high school art teacher, Cincinnati, Ohio

William M. Hudson, elementary school art teacher, Dover, Delaware

Laura L. Hunter, elementary school arts coordinator, Lake City, Florida

Judith A. Jedlicka, Business Committee for the Arts, Inc., New York, New York

Althea Jerome, elementary school music teacher, Hattiesburg, Mississippi

Jonathan Katz, National Assembly of State Arts Agencies, Washington, D.C.

Nicholas S. Kyle, chair, high school fine arts department, Oklahoma City, Oklahoma

John A. Lammel, National Association of Secondary School Principals, Reston, Virginia

Marcia MacCagno Neel, high school choral director, Las Vegas, Nevada

Susan McGreevy-Nichols, middle school dance teacher, Providence, Rhode Island

Theresa Purcell, elementary school physical education/dance teacher, Kendall Park, New Jersey

Judith Rényi, Collaboratives for Humanities and Arts Teaching (CHART), Philadelphia, Pennsylvania

Laura Gardner Salazar, professor of communications, Grand Valley State University, Allendale, Michigan

Acknowledgments

MENC and the Arts Standards Implementation Task Force are grateful to the following organizations for recommending members of the Review Board:
American Alliance for Theatre & Education
American Federation of Teachers
National Art Education Association
National Association of Elementary School Principals
National Dance Association
National Education Association
National Endowment for the Arts

Ordering Information

National Standards for Arts Education. What every young American should know and be able to do in the arts. 1994. ISBN 1-56545-036-1; MENC stock #1605.

Perspectives on Implementation: Arts Education Standards for America's Students. A discussion of the issues related to implementation of the standards and of strategies for key constituencies that need to be involved in the process. 1994. ISBN 1-56545-042-6; MENC stock #1622.

Summary Statement: Education Reform, Standards, and the Arts. A brief statement that spells out the goals of the standards and describes the context from which they emerged. 1994. ISBN 1-56545-037-x; MENC stock #4001 (pack of 10); stock #4001A (single copy).

The Vision for Arts Education in the 21st Century. The ideas and ideals behind the development of the National Standards for Education in the Arts. 1994. ISBN 1-56545-025-6; MENC stock #1617.

Write to MENC Publications Sales, 1806 Robert Fulton Drive, Reston, VA 22091. Credit card holders may call 1-800-828-0229.